SO, YOU WANT TO BECOME A PROFESSIONAL FOOTBALLER?

ADAM WOODAGE WITH RICH LEE

Copyright © AW Publishing 2017
First published in October 2017

All rights reserved.

No part of this publication may be reproduced in any form or by any means - graphic, electronic or mechanical, including photocopying, recording, information storage and retrieval systems without express written permission from the publisher at the address of 6 Chaffinch, Aylesbury, Bucks, HP19 0GQ.

Adam Woodage and Richard Lee have asserted their rights under the Copyright, Design and Patents act of 1988 to be identified as the author (Adam) and subject (Richard) of this work.

The views expressed through this book are those personal to Adam, Richard and the relevant case studies. They are not necessarily relevant to their club, organisation or company's opinion.

Written by: Adam Woodage (AW Publishing)
Designed and covers by: Adam Woodage (AW Publishing)
Printed and bound by: Mixam Printing
Edited by: Rob Paripovic (AW Publishing)
ISBN: 978-0-9935165-7-3

A catalogue record for this book is available from the British Library.

Photo Coverage

To the best of our knowledge, all photos contained within this book are either of the property of Richard Lee or with their permission and right to be reproduced within this publication.

Every effort has been made to trace and contact copyright holders where applicable. If there are any inadvertent omissions we apologise to those concerned, and ask that you contact us so that we can correct any oversight as soon as possible. The contact details are given below:

AW Publishing

6 Chaffinch

Watermead

Aylesbury

Bucks HP19 0GQ

We thank you for your cooperation and understanding within this matter.

CONTENTS

STRONG FOUNDATIONS

PASSION FROM WITHIN - 18

TRIALS - 20

EARLY FOUNDATIONS - 25

THE PARENTAL ROLE - 27

EDUCATION VS FOOTBALL - 31

MAKING THE CUT

FINE MARGINS - 41

YOUNG STARDOM - 44

SACRIFICE - 47

LIFESTYLE RESTRUCTURE - 50

PREHABILITATION - 57

GOAL SETTING - 60

SUSTAINED PERFORMANCE

BOUNCING BACK - 65

ANALYSIS - 68

CONFIDENCE - 71

PRESSURE - 76

GIANTS VS UNDERDOGS - 81

CULTURE OF EXCELLENCE - 85

CULTURE OF EXCELLENCE (SQUAD) - 89

BALANCE - 93

PASSION - 96

WHO IS RICH LEE?

With a career through the ranks of professional football, and now into the world of business and talent development, there are few individuals involved with sport that can boast a CV quite as varied and diverse as Rich. He has always searched for new opportunities to develop and learn, which are greatly mirrored by his achievements and accolades:

PLAYING CAREER
WATFORD FC
BLACKBURN ROVERS FC
FULHAM FC
BRENTFORD FC
BLACKBURN ROVERS FC
ENGLAND U18/U20/U21

ENTREPRENEURIAL ENDEAVOURS
REFUEL PERFORMANCE MANAGEMENT
GK ICON (FAST BECOMING WORLD'S BIGGEST GOALKEEPER COACHING BUSINESS) AND TETRABRAZIL
SKY SPORTS PUNDIT
MOTIVATIONAL SPEAKER

QUALIFICATIONS AND ACCOMPLISHMENTS
MASTER PRACTITIONER IN NEURO-LINGUISTIC PROGRAMMING
FIRST CLASS HONOURS DEGREE IN MEDIA AND JOURNALISM
AUTHOR OF 'GRADUATION: LIFE LESSONS OF A PROFESSIONAL FOOTBALL

FOREWORD

BEN FOSTER

Having known Rich since I joined Watford on loan from Manchester United, it is clear to me that many of the ideologies and philosophies that he stands by have helped to underpin the player that I am today, where I've been fortunate enough to have made in excess of 250 Premier League appearances and have represented my country as well. He speaks of 'controlling the controllable': knowing what you can influence and pumping all of your energy into ensuring that this can be fulfilled.
He speaks of pressure being a state of mind, and a choice, rather than something that is lumped upon us. He speaks of the difficulties involved with becoming a professional footballer, and that everybody does it in

their own, unique way.

Rich has always been, and I believe always will be, a model professional in the way that he gears himself towards continual improvement, and I don't think that there are many other individuals within the world of football who have quite such developed and innovative strategies for dealing with all of the 'baggage' that comes with one of the most highly sought after careers.

We used to spend most afternoons post-training in a coffee shop down the road from the training ground; the discussions that we had were some of the most vivid that I can remember in a period where everything was moving forward at one million miles per hour. We would discuss areas of football, performance and life that were in such a great depth of detail and reflection that it almost seems surreal looking back.

Particularly, Rich used to be infamous around the dressing room for his business ventures away from the game, and I suppose that these only further supported the strength of his mindset and the way in which he was, and always will be, dedicated to achieving success through any form necessary. It certainly has tangible applications to the football field, and I think you will see a lot of these come out through the book. There's no doubt that putting himself through the tribulations of something such as Dragon's Den has massively influenced Rich's personality, and I think that these experiences are testament to the person that Rich is and his desire to push himself beyond his comfort zone.

On that note, the essence of Rich's character is at the forefront of every aspect within this book, and the advice that he gives on a number of different topics is right up there with some of the best advice that I've ever taken in footballing terms. His knowledge of psychology and its application to the reality of professional football is striking, whilst this is successfully warped within the action plans and execution-based evidence that will allow you to put the learnings into practice, whatever your environment.

Knowing that it is as much about a player's 'why' as it is their technical ability, and understanding how all of these elements can work together, Rich certainly has an incredibly holistic approach to his advice for developing talent, and I personally believe that it is this whole picture environment that you need to build as a young player with a chance of success.

I thoroughly enjoyed the opportunity to read his first book, and this publication builds on and develops many of these ideas, whilst integrating them within the context of young footballers, and breaking down the ideas into manageable steps that anyone can follow.

For any young player with a real goal of becoming a professional footballer, this book will act as a vital stepping stone and insight into a world that can often seem very confusing and difficult to understand. It breaks down many complex psychological phenomenons into ideas that all can understand, and beyond that provides the experience, know-how and creative solutions from someone who has been there, understands the journey and works with managing some of the country's best young talent within his performance agency.

I sincerely hope that you enjoy the book and take many messages away from it, regardless of your background or playing career. Take some time to enjoy the pages, reflect on the stories told and think about how they might help you to build and improve on your journey as a player!

All the best,
Ben.

INTRODUCTION

ADAM WOODAGE AND RICHARD LEE

So, you want to become a professional footballer? It might seem a daft question at first: who wouldn't?! And, to a large degree, you're right. There are few careers where you get the opportunity to do that which you love, day-in-day-out, in front of a packed stadium and make the back-page headlines every Sunday. Not to mention, of course, that the pay packet isn't too shabby either.

However, it's no secret that the journey to the top is an incredibly hazardous one, jam-packed with potholes, hidden turnings and dead ends. Not being able to navigate these with the mentality, attitude and mindset of a winner could be the one thing that stops you from reaching that top level. In today's footballing environment, where technical expertise is being pushed to its absolute margins, more and more of the game is coming down to the psychological and mental capabilities of those who step foot on that hallowed turf. Do they 'bottle it' under the pressure? Have they prepared in the best possible way? Is their lifestyle fitting for that of an elite footballer?

The sheer number of variables involved within this journey is mammoth, and it can be so difficult to make the right decisions with little or no knowledge around what you should be doing to give yourself the best chance of success. This, of course, is where we come in. Having experienced the very pinnacle of the footballing pyramid, and now working with some of the country's best young talents with his performance agency, there are few individuals better poised to speak about the lifestyle and psychological choices that young players can make on their way to achieving excellence and developing as a player than Rich. Whether it's teaching you how to deal with pre-match nerves, putting together a training plan for improving your speed or offering advice on how to catch the attention of a local club, Rich has the experience and success in developing programmes and strategies that deliver results and improvements; you can benefit from these too.

Throughout the book, there are opportunities for you to learn, reflect and action upon a variety of topics from goal setting, to dealing with pressure and the debate on education vs football. Using these pages as an inspiration, and platform, for further reading, further development and further improvement is absolutely crucial, and hopefully we've provided you with the framework you need to start to build your own understanding of what performance means to you. You might choose to highlight passages of the book you find particularly useful; you might create a 'cheat sheet' with the best pieces of advice from each section. The reality is that these decisions are for you to make, dependent on what works best for you and will help support that journey towards reaching your full potential.

Over time, you will begin to weed out those that are passionate about making a career from the world of football and those that are simply in it for the next Instagram photo. You will have to make pivotal decisions that will impact your fate and having a strong foundation from which to make these, based on fact, evidence and the science of high performance, will make your job infinitely easier and amplify your chances of making the right decision, in that right moment. It's not to say that the next 120 pages will turn you into the next David Beckham, far from it, but hopefully they will give you the basis from which you can grow as a person and player, having the best possible mindset and attitude towards achieving those levels that you've always dreamed about.

And, at the end of the day, if professional football isn't for you, then the life lessons and strategies that ring true throughout the next twenty chapters will be invaluable to your success, in whatever field your career might lie. Many would argue that playing sport is about learning life lessons. The ability to reflect, to bounce back and to understand what you need to do in order to improve is certainly crucial, and one that we hope to have touched on in plenty of depth through the pages that follow.

In a meantime, if there's one thing that Rich and I can leave you with, it's that the world of football, and elite sport, can be a harsh and unforgiving destiny. It requires hard work, opportunity and continued improvement to even have a chance of making it, and so make sure you enjoy the journey whilst it lasts. Cherish every shot that ruffles the back of the net. Love the feeling of tipping the ball around the post. And never, ever, forget that, when push comes to shove and the day is out, it's just football. It'll still be there tomorrow and you'll almost certainly have another opportunity to prove your worth.

We hope that you find this book as insightful and informative to read as we found it to collaborate upon.

Enjoy the read,
Adam and Rich.

Adam:
Twitter: **@adamwoodage**
Instagram: **@wwwadamwoodagecom**
www.adamwoodage.com

Rich:
Twitter: **@dickielee**
Instagram: **@dickielee01**
www.dickielee.com

SECTION #1

STRONG FOUNDATIONS

1
PASSION FROM WITHIN

Football is a sport that inspires. Whether a player, coach, parent or supporter, the level of ecstasy and euphoria experienced when that net bulges or the goalkeeper palms the ball past the post is unrivalled in nearly all facets in life. It is a powerful vehicle, therefore, in the relationship between a parent and child.

'I think my first footballing memory was being given a Manchester United shirt at Christmas. I was only four or five at the time, and didn't really have much choice in who I was going to support, but there was still a great buzz from being able to wear that infamous badge proudly on my chest', says Rich, with a gleaming smile.

Alongside this initial social involvement with sport, Rich was very quickly developing his desire to play the game, which was manifested - in part - as a result of his father's dedication.

'As a 6-year-old, I joined the U9s at Bedgrove Dynamoes, my father insistent that I would be a left-winger at the time. That was the plan.'

'It mainly happened by luck that I became a goalkeeper. Within the ranks of the club, they were searching for a new goalkeeper for the team (this was very much before the days of position rotation!), and I went for it. Sadly, another 'keeper was chosen ahead of me and that could well have been the end of this story. After just one game, though, he got bored and I got my opportunity to pit myself between the sticks and the affinity grew from there.'

Much of football might have changed since these times, but I ask Rich whether any of his earlier footballing experiences sit particularly strongly in his memory. 'There was one game that I can recall, probably only my fifth or sixth game ever, because it grew my desire to play football even further. It was against Belgrave, and we were 1-0 down when the opposition got a penalty. The striker struck the ball low to my left, and I went down and managed to hold onto the ball. At the time, I remembered it as a fiercely struck penalty that zipped across the deck. Applying a bit of logic to that (and remembering it was the shot of an 8-year-old!) it probably wasn't quite so venomous.'

'We then went up the other end, scored two goals and proceeded to win the game 2-1.' Even now, it is clear that Rich is getting that buzz of being the hero on the football pitch, and so I question him on it further. 'The core of the memory has revolved around seeing my dad as proud as he was, the excitement of my teammates on the sidelines and the general euphoria that follows a stand-out moment on the football pitch.'

If we apply some basic principles to this, it becomes clear that Rich was extrinsically motivated to perform in this case by a number of key factors. It is common for footballers to perform well under situations of 'social facilitation', and Rich's desire to please and live up to the expectations of his parents and teammates certainly fits within that bracket.

'Even at this point, I think that there was a subconscious and implicit understanding that it was a vehicle through which I could impress my dad, which was massive for me. I look at it now as a 34-year-old, and I don't think it was ever the love of football that took me into the game. It was more the feelings that were generated through the game, and the fact that it could be an incredible mechanism for pleasing people from there.'

'There wasn't much goalkeeper-specific training at Bedgrove, other than the dad on the sideline who would volley a few balls my way from time-to-time. The trial and journey at Watford started at around the age of 10 or 11, and obviously there was more in the way of a goalkeeper coach there.'

2

TRIALS

There aren't too many footballers, a minuscule percentage of those playing the game, in fact, that will ever have the opportunity to undertake a trial for a professional football club. With the recruitment as developed as it is now, though, many players are being involved in trials from a younger age. On reflection, Rich believes that being given this opportunity at a young age was a stepping stone in terms of his development, as opposed to a hurdle he had to navigate.

'Getting my trial at Watford was pure luck. One of the parent helpers from Bedgrove Dynamoes also happened to be a scout for Watford, running one of their Centre of Excellence academies. He came to watch a game that we were playing in, and made a number of recommendations from there. Unfortunately, I wasn't one of those recommendations… It might have had something to do with the fact that we won 10-0 and that I'd barely touched the ball! However, my dad had a word with my manager, who subsequently had a word with the scout, and all of a sudden I was invited along to an extended trial.'

'There were 70 kids and seven goalkeepers to start off with, and numbers dropped every week. I was lucky enough to be kept on through the entire process, and I do put a lot of it down to luck: you're at the mercy of a selection team who might naturally be biased or mistaken in their decision-making. They don't see your entire game, just small snippets that could reflect positively or negatively on you.'

At the start of any trial period, it is difficult for players to know what's expected of them, or how things might turn out. This is reflected in their emotions. 'I was nervous, without a doubt', Rich says. 'But if I think back to when I was 10, 11 and 12 years old, I didn't feel the nerves quite so much as I did as an older player, and I think a lot of young players will be similar to me in that regard. For me, it's down to the fact that the experiences of football that you have at that age are mainly positive, and you haven't necessarily built an arsenal of negative feelings and fear that could dislodge that. If anything, it was just joy and wanting to go and play football.'

Certainly in the modern day, where the quality and environment that grassroots football is being coached in is improving, this is an idea that seems to make logical sense: if you don't have any worries about your position in football or your confidence, then you, surely, will not be too nervous about the opportunity to play at a higher level. In fact, confidence is likely to blossom as you become more comfortable with the environment, as it did for Rich during his experiences.

'As each week of the trial process moved forward, I grew more and more confident. There was a point at which one of the coaches pulled my parents aside after a training session and asked if they could take me along to the academy sessions as well, which supported my development hugely and helped me feel considerably more comfortable in the trials. You have this strange realisation that you're progressing. I found it quite early on, and I will always recall one of the coaches asking how tall my dad was (6"5), and that was enough for them to be confident in their decision of signing me on.'

'It's a lot more technical now, and it's not quite so simple', Rich tells me. It was at this point, though, that his initial forage into the professional game of football was well and truly underway, even though he might have been sceptical in the early stages.

Given this difficulty in the modern day, Rich and I discuss what players can do to give themselves the best chances of being selected. His ideas mimic, almost, that of searching for a job. 'If you're putting in the efforts to become a top footballer, and you know that you're not being seen out there at the moment, then you have to take a proactive approach. It's a case of reaching out to people locally who have contacts in the clubs, building up a CV of your footballing-related experiences and successes, and not being afraid to ask for trials.'

'Clubs don't want to miss out on the next Lionel Messi or the next Peter Schmeichel, so more often than not they will at least look at you and give you the opportunity to prove yourself. And if it doesn't work out? Try somewhere else. Continue to improve the whole time, because wherever you are is merely a vehicle and platform for where you want to go. We've all got the aspirations of being in the Premier League or playing for our country, and I'll often tell my young players not to be down if they're not in the position that they want to be in just yet. It is just a vehicle. The club that you're at will allow you to improve, as will the players you're with. If you've got the ability and, more importantly, the attitude, then you will make it to the best level.'

If the club you're with at present is a vehicle, then, it is being as positive, proactive and committed as possible to taking that vehicle forward, knowing that once you reach a point you will have the opportunity to search for a new one, that seems to underlines Rich's visions and philosophies about carving that career.

ACTION PLAN

We've already likened the process of trying to get a trial to one similar to writing a CV, and it doesn't just stop there. In the digital world, where anyone can speak to anyone at the drop of the hat, there are plenty of ways that we can search for trials and stand-out in our quest for being seen by the top clubs.

Look for open trial days

Many clubs offer some form of open trials, which are available to any player who thinks that they might be good enough to deal with an elite setting. These are usually held ahead of a new season, and are an excellent experience to become more comfortable with the trial environment and also to see how you compare against other players of a similar age. And, of course, there's a chance you may be invited back at the end of it!

Build a 'football CV'

We've spoken about it briefly already, but a football CV could be one of the most helpful assets (especially for slightly older players) in helping you to be differentiated from your competition. You can include things like clubs previously played for, tournaments involved in, or even your previous coaches. It's all about helping a club to see why you might have the potential to be an asset to their team, and is another path to getting yourself that trial.

Contact recruitment/scouting departments

Depending on the size and nature of the club, there will be either a couple of departments or a couple of staff members dedicated to unearthing young talent and bringing it into the organisation. Usually, the contact details for these individuals are published online, or in some other location. Finding these, and making individualised contact to different clubs explaining why you could be of benefit to that team is a great and direct way to get infront of those who will ultimately make the final decisions.

Video footage

The theme of video footage features a number of times in this book, primarily from a reflection and analysis perspective. However, it is also a vital addition to any CV, or other application to a trial. Get a tripod and video a few of your matches and training sessions, putting the highlights up on a private YouTube video that you can then share with the relevant scouts to help bolster your application.

Play out of your skin!

Regardless of how much you do to build up a reputation or network with local scouts, you will ultimately be determined by your performances on the pitch. There is simply no room for failure here. Put in the extra hours on the training ground, dedicate yourself to performing the best you can and your results will pay off relative to that.

EARLY FOUNDATIONS

Every season, the game of football is becoming more and more appreciative of the physiological and technical principles that can be built around the early stages of an athlete's development. Speak to any professional footballer, and you will almost always notice a pattern that emerges, with various fundamental movement and motor skills being built up through their early years that would prove to be the platform for future stardom. It comes up in conversation between Rich and I, with the trademark signals still an ever-present feature.

'I found that, without even focussing on it massively, I was in an environment where I was undertaking incredible amounts of unstructured play and practice, which was child-led and contributing to my development.' Whilst much of Malcolm Gladwell's extrapolation of the '10,000 hours' rule has been critiqued of late, there's no denying that the more practice a developing athlete can undertake, the greater their chances of achieving success. 'I had certain motivations that meant that every opportunity I had to play football within school I would take, whether that be at lunchtime, before school, after school, or within the curriculum itself. On top of that, as soon as I returned home I'd have a ball of some description in my hands, and would be finding a way to use it. I remember that there was a ridge underneath my sofa that I could roll the ball against to practice my low-diving saves, whilst there was a beam in one of the rooms that I'd throw the ball against to practice cross-taking and dealing with a ball at height.'

'Doing the maths, I imagine that there was probably around three to four hours of unstructured activity taking place every evening when I was younger, and that certainly has contributed to my development, alongside the practice at clubs. Your game is nestled within hundreds and thousands of small details and variations of movement patterns - if you can improve yourself across any number of these areas by a significant margin, you will be well on your way to achieving the greatest level of excellence that you can reach.'

It is a fascinating theme personally and one where you can only step back and question how growing cultural and social trends (such as children spending more time inside on games consoles) will influence the quality of footballers in a generation or two down the line. For parents, or athletes, who are looking to kindle this intrinsic motivation to engage in play and practice, sometimes the biggest returns can be found in things as simple as encouraging the use of footballs, tennis balls and balloons, whether this be against a wall within the house, against a sofa in a 'breakables-free' lounge or in the garden: setting up the environment is the lion-share of the work!

THE PARENTAL ROLE

When I ask Rich about the influence he believes that parents have in the success of young athletes, his message to those who want to create a career is simple, straight and succinct: 'You're never going to do this on your own'.

'If you're a parent reading this, you have to understand that your involvement will be crucial to your child's success, especially in the way that the academy system works in the modern day. I was incredibly lucky that I had a mum who would drive me two hours to training, however many times a week, and sit in the car whilst I was there, just so I could have the best possible chance of achieving success. If it wasn't for that, I wouldn't be sat here now talking about my experiences of playing top-flight football!' Your support team, in that regard, is massive, believes Rich, but they also play a huge role in inspiring that initial spark within a youngster's mind.

Recalling his childhood once more, I ask Rich about his favourite footballing memories; it is interesting to see the facilitative role that his parents played within these. 'As a kid, I supported Manchester United because they were my dad's team. We went everywhere to watch them, including a trip to the Camp Nou, which is a memory that holds particularly strong.' As Rich describes this in more detail, the innocent and unfiltered emotions of childhood football beam from his persona and voice. 'It was during the times of Yorke and Cole - I could never forget their infamous step-over and one-two routine that they performed exquisitely that evening. The match was full of entertainment and excitement, with three goals a piece shared between some of the world's greatest players. I will never forget the feeling of standing next to my dad, on the highest tier of that enormous stadium, singing my heart out until my voice was coarse without a care in the world.' Memories that many children will have of the wonderful game, but only possible because of the work and opportunities created by those who guide them in their early footballing journeys. At the same time, later down the line, the emotions that parents have to deal with inside the game of football, and especially for those who are fortunate enough to be involved within the academy setup, can sit at the polar opposite.

Knees jangling, sweat running down his face and a feeling of dread engulfing Rich's stomach, he gingerly crept down the stairs of his Buckinghamshire country home and into the lounge. 'What I was about to tell my dad would break his heart, I knew it, and the guilt I felt at this point was overwhelming: I was struggling to control my emotions. I remember how purely miserable I felt, and I didn't know how much longer I could wilfully sustain it.' Hesitantly, Rich stuttered the words 'Dad, I don't want to play football anymore…'

One of the most difficult moments for any young footballer can be the changing and rollercoaster-esque emotions and affinities that they have towards the game of football. At this point in time, Rich was 14 years old, signed to Watford FC and very highly thought of amongst both his coaches and the academy staff. The journey that led to this conversation formed some of his toughest times in football. 'By my own admission, my relationship with football wasn't a positive one, even at this young age. I didn't connect with too many of my teammates, and seemed to spend the majority of the game dreading the rollicking that would often accompany another thrashing.' It was probably the first time that Rich asked himself whether he was cut out for professional football.

'I could see Dad was upset, but the advice that he offered me held me in incredibly good stead moving forward. His words proved fruitful and are something that I'm very thankful for. I truly believe that he understood that it wasn't his job to make the decision for me, either way, but instead to help me consider all of the pros and cons in an objective and measured manner.'

Knowing that it was March and that the season was soon to come to a close, Rich's dad (Peter) advised him that he should simply see the season out and spend the summer mulling over his options. 'At the time of this conversation, I was experiencing one of my toughest times as a goalkeeper: we'd had three heavy defeats on the bounce, which included an 8-1 drubbing by QPR. There's no doubt that it had left me fragile, and I think that Dad appreciated that I was in no position to make a life-altering decision.'

With this story in mind, (the outcome of which led to Rich rediscovering his passion for the game after a summer away) I ask what Rich says to the parents of the athletes he works with, and what general advice he would give to those empowered with the opportunity to support their child's development.

'As a parent, your job is actually quite a simple one: support your child. This doesn't mean that you need to tell him or her that they're the next best thing, papering over any cracks in their lifestyle or game, but it does mean helping them up when they're feeling down and reminding them that you'll support them regardless of their levels of performance. If your child is destined for the top reaches of professional football, they will feel enough pressure and desire as it is; having parents breathing down their neck may well be the tipping point.'

Rich speaks in great detail on many occasions about the emotions that many young footballers will experience and strive for; does he believe these can be felt through to the parents as well?

'Of course: it's natural to have high hopes for your child. It's natural to have your own dreams attached to their success - what parent wouldn't love the thought of sitting at Wembley watching their pride and joy perform in front of thousands of spectators?'

It is crucial, though, that parents can have the ability to recognise and understand the manifestation of these raw emotions, and ensure that they are channelled positively and in moderation towards their children. 'It's incredibly healthy to have a parent that can motivate you to achieve success, and is equally committed to your levels of success, but there must be a realisation of when 'supportive' becomes 'pushy': it's these moments where parents could be doing more harm than good, without even realising it.'

EDUCATION VS FOOTBALL

How much time should I take away from education in order to give myself the best chance of footballing success? The question is asked in head of years' offices throughout the country, generally met by a level of disappointment from the student involved and a teacher that explains the frightfully poor odds of 'making it' as a professional footballer. Rich, though, takes a different stance on the age-old balance that must be struck by the two learning experiences.

'This is something that not everyone will agree with me on. I fully appreciate that the statistics say that, very simply, the chances that you will make it as a professional footballer are minuscule. Therefore, many would abide by the law of averages in this regard, and believe that you should focus on education: that is the safest bet for fulfilling a comfortable career. Having said that, many psychologists and performance experts in the world hold true their common sense beliefs that the more time, focus and energy that you give any activity, the greater the eventual likelihood is that you will become an expert within that domain.'

'When it comes to football', Rich says 'the margins are so tight that individuals who find themselves spending half their time on education and half their time on sport may actually be the orchestrator of their own failure: they will almost certainly fall behind somebody who had less of a chance of making it as a footballer but is capable and prepared to spend 80% or 90% of their time working towards it. People speak about individuals such as Wayne Rooney, who many accept may not have the highest levels of cognitive or academic intelligence, but his spatio-temporal and footballing intelligence is incredible - there's no doubt that the amount of time he's spent on the football pitch has contributed massively to that. As a kid, he fully immersed himself in the game of football and his personal development.'

To solidify this viewpoint, Rich adds some anecdotal evidence from within his performance agency. 'I remember a conversation that I had with a young lad not too long ago, and it is probably a theme that underlines the world of football at present. He has all the physical attributes he'll ever need to play the game at the highest level, and would fit within the ideal checklist that many clubs are starting to formulate these days. In essence, I said to him that if he can dedicate himself 100% to football between now and the age of 34, with no distractions away from the game or pitfalls to be caught up in, he's got an incredible chance to go on and play for England, or at least in the Premier League.' The difficulty, without a doubt, is in the execution, especially with so many of the external pressures and stereotypical conventions that modern players are subject to.

'Of course: I'm not naïve into ignoring the potential pitfalls. Football is a sink or swim environment where you'll either become a multi-millionaire world-star very quickly, or you could find yourself spiralling out of the game in your late teens without any career backing, formal qualifications or idea as to what direction you could possibly take next. That's the truth of it.'

'I'm not saying that you need stellar A-levels or seven years of conventional education in order to be successful and achieve the career that you desire outside of football, but it can become very demoralising for young players who fall out of the game and are a number of steps behind their peers in terms of approaching the workplace and finding themselves a job. It's something that players must be aware of, and consider heavily in their decision as to whether they want to be a professional footballer, because the only realistic way to achieve optimum success is to go all out, and players must be conscious of the potential repercussions of this later down the line.'

There certainly are steps that players take during their footballing development that may not interfere with their progress, helping to ensure and secure the possibility of a career beyond the game. A lot of time as a footballer is spent in rest and recovery, and Rich believes that these are excellent opportunities to really plough forward with homework, studying or whatever additional work can be completed in order to provide you with some kind of qualification alongside your footballing journey. 'Certainly, there will be a point where many players reduce their level of study as they edge ever closer to the margins that are required for the professional reaches of the game, so taking your own personal initiative and ownership over your education is massive at this point. It can help you protect and negate some of the potential issues that could arise. This has no consequence or influence on your football: you can still perform and train to your absolute limits, but you're just utilising that rest time to the best of your ability and not allowing it to go as wasted time'.

'Another way to think about it is to consider looking at your life in proportions', suggests Rich. 'It's all about finding the ratio of football to education (as well as other aspects of your life) that works best for you. We'll talk about achieving a balance further down the line, but it can be as simple as thinking about the percentage of time that you can dedicate to football alongside education, how this might change over the years and what this ultimately looks like on a day-to-day basis. Some people might find that balance at 70/30, others at 60/40 or 90/10, whilst there will be the occasional sensation who can work at a 50/50 balance between football and education, but still have the ability and focus when necessary to carve themselves a career out of the game.'

It's a decision that has to be made early: something that's personable, informed, and individual to each player. Rich speaks even further about the importance of it being proactive. 'If it's a reactive tactic that's used at a crisis point, it's much less likely that it'll be a rational decision and you may well find that the time during which it would have been most useful has already passed. Having that ability to dictate and be aware of your own priorities is a massive skill in itself, so the proactive approach is imperative to me in that sense.'

The bottom line for Rich, though, is that as much as you can push yourself to the maximum of creating that career for yourself, you should take every opportunity that comes your way. 'It's easy to set yourself on a path of moderation, allowing the ability to float from football, to education, to whatever else might emerge as an excuse, almost, for not reaching or approaching your goals, when you know that it would have been possible if you'd thrown your heart and soul into it.'

'At the end of the day, how much will you really value that A in RE if it has potentially prevented you from achieving a career in professional football, with a multi-million pound contract every year and the joy of playing in front of 60,000 fans?'

Rich uses the analogy of a golf shot. 'Imagine you're trying to hit the ball onto the green from 150 yards on the fairway, and you know that you can hit the shot successfully in your sleep, every single time. All of a sudden, you realise that there's a bunker to the left of the hole, water on the far side of the green and a line of trees to the right. Usually, at this point, a multitude of decisions would start racing through your mind: should I play short and safe? What about playing the ball into the bunker?

How can I make sure I avoid the pitfalls?'

'It's easy, at this point, to hit the safe option, and play the ball conservatively in whatever fashion that might be, but those with real strength of character and who will ultimately be most successful are those with the ability to have trust in their skill level and potential, going all out to hit the green that they know they can reach.'

In sum, then, Rich says: 'it's a case of not worrying about the pitfalls or the distractions until absolutely necessary, knowing that you've got the ability to be creative and enterprising in bouncing back if things go wrong and you miss the shot; having this confidence is crucial. You can transfer this very strongly across to the world of football, in my opinion: are you letting the distractions and hazards overrule your behaviour, or having the trust in your own focus, determination and potential to achieve success?'

The conversation with Rich subsequently moves on to the way in which that he dealt with the ongoing battle during his early days as a player. With both of us being students at Aylesbury Grammar School, Rich's GCSE studies seemed a suitable starting point. 'Exams for me were a very difficult point with regards to the realisation of how much time I should be devoting to my life outside of football. In the end, I think that my levels of self-awareness and efficiency helped me most in getting through the period with very 'good value' grades (in terms of achievement vs time dedicated).'

'I ended up taking around the month in the run up to exam period off from football, because I thought it was sufficiently important to giving me some kind of cushion behind the sport, but beyond that I managed to achieve large levels of success in my football that year through following some simple principles and ideas. Firstly, I was very conscious that every minute counted. I was focussed during school hours and ensured that I got as much done during the day as I could, as well as being efficient with homework so as always to complete it, but to focus on the exam-relevant information that I would have to be able to recall.'

'On top of that, I had a massive determination that I was going to make the tandem of football and education work for a period of time. I used to get into school at about 7:30AM every morning, and spend an hour revising and finishing off homework before the day started, instead of chatting to my mates as the majority of the group would do; this proved an incredible tool to me in allowing me to complete large amounts of work, without the distractions or bustle of the evening schedule. It didn't impact my football in any significant manner.'

From this perspective, there's little doubt that Rich had one clear priority in his former years: football. Using the time he had around him to the maximum level of efficiency would prove to be a crucial mechanism in ensuring his success, and the beauty of this kind of process is that it's applicable to any young footballer determined in succeeding on the pitch but without allowing everything else to enter free-fall. It's all about being creative and innovative in finding the structures that work most efficiently for you outside of football, and using these to increase the number of hours that you can spend on the football pitch. As Rich concludes: 'being efficient in everything that I did was the underlying theme, I believe, and that meant that I could ensure that football was not negatively influenced during the periods where maybe there was more pressure to make schooling my priority'.

ACTION PLAN

This is an area where design can pay off massively for young athletes. We've included the following questions to help probe your plans a little bit more, and help you to figure out where your priorities really lie:

School career

1) How many years do I have left in education?
2) What am I hoping to do once I finish my education?
3) What steps do I need to take to achieve this?

Playing career

1) How many hours of football am I currently playing per week?
2) Do I need to be spending more hours playing organised football?
3) How could I integrate a potential education within my football?

Current lifestyle

1) What proportion of my time am I spending on football vs education?
2) How am I currently using my rest and recovery periods?
3) During what activities am I most productive with my work?

Changing your lifestyle

1) Which three areas of my lifestyle could I improve efficiency in most?

2) What steps can I take to achieve the football/education ratio I've decided on?

3) How can I utilise my free time more effectively?

Reflection (after a given period)

1) How are the changes that I've made supporting my development?

2) How do I feel, physically and mentally, with my new workload?

3) Are there any further ways in which I believe that I can develop?

SECTION #2
MAKING THE CUT

6
FINE MARGINS

Margins are becoming finer every day in the footballing world. With the amount of money and levels of technology wrapped around the modern game, there is simply no getting away from the performance-based orientation of the game, and this can have large implications for the careers of young footballers. Whether it's within a successful trial, being offered your first professional contract or nestling yourself into the senior side, marginal differences define a large part of the game we play. And these differences, of course, have a butterfly effect on the future that we can carve for ourselves, as Rich explains through the story of his debut. 'The story of my debut is a perfect example of the margins that exist within the game of football; one inch can be the difference.'

'I was about 19 or 20 at the time' Rich tells me, playing for Watford. 'I remember that we'd lost on the Saturday before, and Neal Ardley (one of the senior pros who's now manager at AFC Wimbledon) decided that he wanted to take me on a night out; I wasn't going to say no to one of the top dogs in the dressing room! We had a real fun night and a great time, and went in for training again on the Sunday. My coach and I had a great relationship and he was always keen to know about what we got up to on a night out, which was why I was particularly confused when he was rather blunt about the matter at training that morning. He just didn't seem impressed at all.'

At this point, Rich was stumped by the change of perspective from his coach. Looking back, he realises that it was the earliest indication of his debut being on the way. 'It wasn't until the Tuesday of the game that I understood his bemusement, because I was collared by the manager during the pre-match analysis and told that I'd be playing that evening, as he wanted to rest the main goalkeeper for an upcoming cup match. It explained the staleness, without a doubt!'

Instantly, the nerves hit and were coupled with a cocktail of excitement and anxiousness for the game ahead. 'The first half was pretty average, we went 1-0 down to a penalty, and Sean Dyche had managed to get himself sent off, but there wasn't a lot that I had to do other than that', Rich recalls. 'It was two minutes into the second half, though, where there was a very defining moment that could have had an incredible and forever-lasting impact on my career: a routine shot came in after the opposition had cut inside and had a shot. As I went to take the ball above my head, it somehow slipped through my hands, flicked onto the crossbar and headed over the net for a corner. If you could ever personify a heart-in-mouth moment, that was it. I thought that the world was about to come crashing down on me in that moment.'

Testament to Rich's character now, though, he managed to bounce back strongly from the escapade and would proceed to have a blinding second-half. 'I went on to make four decent saves and was awarded Man of the Match for the tie. From this point, I was given occasional opportunities to play over the next few months, and excelled in my performance within these'. Rich was included in the England U21 squad that summer. The significance of this debut, though, - or the reason that Rich reflects on it so deeply - was that there was another player making his debut for the club on the day, who was held in similar regards to Rich in developmental terms; the two had an almost identically projected path at the club. 'He was substituted on the 60th minute', Rich tells me, 'after a less than spectacular appearance in the opinion of the management, and would never play for the club again. He continued to fall out of the professional game at this point, and ended up grafting in the non-league scene for many years, without ever making that transition back into the Football League.'

By contrast, Rich's career snowballed from his debut and he went on to make waves throughout the English leagues. 'Fortunately, on the other hand, I went on to play a couple of hundred games for various clubs, including a stint in the Premier League during my career. It does make you sit back and consider just how fine the margins are in football.'

'I look back very often and can't help but wonder what might have happened had the crossbar been an inch higher that afternoon: if I'd conceded that goal, proceeded to have a poor second half and not started for the club for a long time following the match, would I have had the future opportunities that I was granted to make a career for myself, or might I be following a similar journey in the reaches of non-league football?'

At the end of the day, it is impossible to tell how much of a butterfly effect Rich's debut had, or didn't have, on his career. A realisation that margins are very prominent within the game of football is vital for parents and players, not just from the perspective of maximising them, but also with the understanding and acceptance that achieving perfection is a futile and trivial task: it simply will not be met in a game with so many external variables that no-one can control. As Rich and I will consider to discuss further through the book, however, how players react to and build upon the fine margins they encounter will play, potentially, the biggest part in building their holistic career.

7
YOUNG STARDOM

Flash cars. Expensive watches. Newspaper back pages. It's not difficult to see, nor understand, why young footballers can so often be sucked in and sucker-punched by the temptation of fame and stardom within the game of football. Especially with the recent advent of even further inflated broadcasting deals, transfer fees and supposed 'comfort levels' for many young players, the mental strength and awareness required to navigate that ship away from the hidden rocks is one of the most overlooked skills in the game of football. At the very top level, inordinate funds are pumped into mentoring, managing and gestating these potential '£100 million assets' (and yet even these efforts don't produce perfect results), but through the lower professional steps of the game, this can be a massive stepping stone and one that Rich has experienced first-hand.

'If you do manage to get the point in your career where you're making a professional debut for any sizeable club, you certainly have to be very aware of the 'hype' that runs alongside this, especially in the modern game with the growth of social media and the like', Rich explains to me, very early on in our conversation. 'When I made my debut for Watford, I think that I struggled with this aspect of the game. After playing a few games, you don't really consider how many people know who you are. As your career grows, you might have a gauge by the number of followers you have on Twitter or Instagram, but at these early points it can be quite shocking and surprising to see the sheer extent of people who recognise you.'

Rich remembers, particularly, a night out in Watford after he'd made a couple of starts for the club. 'I was regularly approached by fans asking for a photo, my autograph, and all the general behaviours that surround someone when they meet a footballer. There's always a danger for that young footballer that a sense of power and status can go to their head, and that's very risky: it's not real.'

'Despite the fact that you might seem the centre of attention in that moment, you will be quickly forgotten if you can't achieve a sense of longevity within your career and build a name for yourself.'

I ask Rich, then, what kind of impacts these distractions can have on the game of young players. 'Naturally, when things are going very well and you're in a positive place, it can become more difficult to focus once more on the essential and basic tasks within the game, often leading to players forgetting about the behaviours that got them to that positive place in the first place.'

On top of this, Rich sees the build-up of positivity an almost sure-fire prediction that the clouds will come tumbling down over time. 'It's almost as if a lot of this speculation can build you up to shoot you down.' 'Everyone is so positive at first, and desperate for the local lad to do well, but there's always a time where this shifts, and I think I saw that during my early years in the game as well.'

'All of a sudden, I was being insulted and criticised by fans on the forums, who I'd never met before, with the seemingly sole aim of generating a bit of disruption. They'd call me all kinds of things on social media, as well as making up stories about me online and I did not know how to deal with it. At the time, I didn't have the capacity to know how to deal with the situations I was in, and ended up being quite frustrated and depressed as a result. It's a vicious circle, because you can obviously understand the subsequent influence that it would have on my performance.'

It was the negative comments during Rich's career that stayed with him most memorably, and this is something that all players must be able to deal with. 'Even to this day, I can recall word-for-word some of my criticisms from the forums, but I've got absolutely no idea of any of the positive feedback the fans might have given me. The mind can have a funny way of manipulating you like this.

For many of the young players that Rich and his team work with, this can be an issue of real concern. 'Especially when they've made big money moves, with the girls, cars and stardom following them, it's often an incredibly difficult job for us to steer that ship back towards the end goal and ensure that focus and commitment doesn't drop as a result of the surroundings. In England especially, where there's such a strong league system with an abundance of cash on tap for players, we see so many players who don't achieve their full potential because they become comfortable with achieving some of their goals early on, and subsequently living the glamorous lifestyle from that point onwards.' These are wise and insightful words from Rich, who clearly understands the potential hazards that young players can face.

8

SACRIFICE

It is quite categorical: you will not make it to the top without a number of innate drives, sacrifices and mindsets. Whilst football may be a non-linear game, that encourages individual freedom and expression, one underlying principle of those who make it through the talent pathway is that they sacrifice along the way. Rich, in his career and with those that he works with, sees it no differently, and adds that there must be an intrinsic desire to love and play the game.

'In terms of personal system management and sacrifices, the first thing that I will say is that it has to be a choice that you want to make. Given the professionalism of the modern game, there is no wriggle-room to live the George Best lifestyle and still perform in the leagues of English football. You just can't do it. The standard is too high'.

'If you dream of playing at the highest level, you have to make a conscious and willing choice towards the way that you're going to train, manage your lifestyle and perform in order to maximise your form', Rich adds. 'The reality of it is that many people will say that they've made this choice, and maybe kick up a great fuss about how committed they are to the process, but their actions may not necessarily be aligned with that: execution is the most difficult part, without a doubt.' One of the biggest questions that Rich is asked within his agency and beyond runs along the lines of 'what is that sacrifice?'.

He believes that it's a combination of factors that mould together to kindle a burning desire to play:

Passion for the game - This is all about your passion and dedication to the game: wanting to spend every breathing minute examining, playing and discovering its nuances. There can't be any negotiation on that, and you've got to find a way to fit a substantial amount of it into your schedule.

Alcohol - Another obvious one, especially in 2017. It would be naïve of me to say that players in the modern day don't drink at all, but I think that the idea of the drunken footballer in the modern day is dead. I don't think there's any footballer at the top of the Premier League that you'd see going into Alcoholics Anonymous, because they just wouldn't survive the demanding physical margins of their career. It's a decision that you have to make very early on in your career, and the temptations of peer pressure and nights out will often be difficult to handle, but you only have to look at the scientific evidence to see the damage that it can do to your body.

Sleep - This is a massively important facet that I think can be overlooked from time-to-time. Having regular sleep periods and patterns is imperative to your levels of rest and recovery, and you see a lot of money being pumped in by clubs to facilitate this in the modern day: if you can't fit to this as a footballer then you're really going to struggle. Just look at something like the facilities of Manchester City (where there is a purpose-built complex with individualised sleeping and recovery rooms for players after home matches/training) to see the growing impact that this will have on the modern game.

Nutrition - This is vital, once more. There's so much more out there than there used to be and we can see the evidence of the impact that it has on injuries, training levels and performance. A footballer simply can't neglect the impact that diet will have on their energy levels, because so many of their rivals and competitors will make massive gains from these areas.

Media - An interesting one, because we certainly don't want to encourage the creation of robots in the modern world, but it's imperative that you feed your mind with information that is going to inspire, stimulate and motivate you to achieve more. It's about always learning and continual development. You've always got to be moving forward and seeking improvement: this could be the difference between being a League Two or Championship player a couple of years down the line.

In short, then, here are just five areas where players will have to adjust their lifestyle and potentially make some difficult choices if they want the best chance of stepping onto that hallowed turf. However, Rich thinks it can be counter-intuitive and unproductive at times to view these areas as sacrifices: they are merely the means through which a growth mindset must be nurtured. 'I think that we bed all of these areas of our lifestyle under the term 'sacrifice', but it's much more about taking a positive and proactive outlook to the way in which you acquit yourself. It has to be a lifestyle that you enjoy living, if you want any chance of achieving longevity within the systems you're creating; this is the point at which many players fall down.'

'It's easy to be committed for a week, a month, even a season when you're playing well and performing at your best. Those who have the longest and most fulfilling careers, though, (a la Ryan Giggs) are the ones who can continue that commitment as a habit from the start of their career and right the way through.'

9
LIFESTYLE RESTRUCTURE

Margins. Systems. Lifestyle. Expectations. Sacrifice. Throughout the course of even the early sections of this book, we've spoken about so many areas to the young player's pathway that must be optimised if they want to reach their peak and achieve all that is possible. Being able to talk the talk is one thing, though, and we all know that the results come in the execution. Rich and I speak about how you can turn these variables into real, actionable improvements. 'The first port of call is to know where you're at, and have a real honest evaluation of your development', Rich begins. 'If you're of the opinion that there's nothing that you can improve, then I can make a judgement with clarity straight away: you will not become a professional footballer. It's that simple.'

'Even Lionel Messi and Cristiano Ronaldo have areas in which they can improve and work tirelessly to achieve them. The fact that they know that is why they continue to improve and find incredible levels of excellence in everything they do.' Rich is often asked how one can achieve this by the young players in his agency, and many of the ideas are similar messages to those we've discussed. 'For me, the first step is to break down your game and lifestyle into as many little pieces as you can, and then assess the areas where you can make the biggest marginal gains. It could be as simple as a change of diet, allocating free-time to read a certain book or changing your morning routine; you'll be surprised by the incredible returns that these can build over time. With a hyper-focus, whether that be towards an aspect of your game or your lifestyle, so much is possible.'

'I often like to use the example of training the weaker foot. This is a brilliant technical ability that we can isolate and work on individually without our team more often than some other skills, so is a great way to improve our margins as a player. If you want to be a top player in any position, you can't have a weak foot anymore: there are too many others who have trained themselves to become as close to ambidextrous as possible. Having that intention to go out and undertake purposeful practice towards improving this margin of your game is massive, and it might not be that you do it alone. You have to have the confidence to reach out to the experts when you're looking at how you can become more efficient, productive and successful in what you do.'

And, for Rich, knowing that he had an area he needed to improve was all it would require to take the necessary steps outside of his comfort zone and achieve those improvements. 'One summer, whilst at Watford in my early years, I remember that I wanted to improve my kicking. My first step was, over the off-season, to reach out to a number of top goalkeepers who might be able to help me with their experience and expertise. Sadly, this came to no avail, but some more research allowed me to find a contact for Jonny Wilkinson's kicking coach: Dave Alred. Dave had an MBE, received after Wilkinson kicked through the posts against Australia, and had generally built up a great name for himself in the world of rugby and sport as a whole (he also supported Luke Donald on his journey to the top-ranked golfer in the world). I was truly fascinated by him.'

'So, what did you do first?', I ask Rich.

'I gave him a ring and asked him how much it would cost for a session. It's fair to say I was a little bit shocked at his price tag of £5,000 a day...!'

It seemed as though that door was closed before it even opened, but the world has an interesting way of working things out. 'Lo and behold, when I came back to training for pre-season, on the first day Dave had turned up at the training ground.' Totally unrelated to Rich's endeavours,

Aidy Boothroyd (then manager of Watford) had hired Dave to come down and give all the goalkeepers a kicking workshop and session.

'It went down really well for me,' Rich remarked 'and got me in the manager's good books at an important part of my development, especially when Dave explained the situation to him!'

Whilst the level of performance and expertise that Dave held may not be directly transferable to the support that all young players can receive, Rich and I still speak about the benefit that it brought to his game. 'The session was perfect for me. The tips and advice that he gave me were mind-blowing. I knew that the advice I was taking on was coming from a credible source, and therefore that it would help me be the very best that I could be: I had full and total faith in it.'

It's key, in Rich's opinion, to start to vet the advice that you're taking, as soon as there are multiple voices on the table. 'Don't listen to any armchair football fan who's never played football and has no understanding of how the game works. It's not a case of over-valuing experience, but it's a case of tapping into the knowledge fountains of those who have achieved, or worked with athletes, at the top level, ideally someone you admire and respect greatly.'

In Rich's process of achieving development through these learning experiences, this is just the first step, however. 'The next task is to be a sponge: listen to and absorb all the information that you can possibly extract from your interactions, and think on a very deep level about how you can integrate it into your game. From this point, it's a case of executing and practicing that advice time and time again, making sure that repetition is achieved through variation.'

'And, of course', Rich adds 'you will use different people for different aspects of your game: would I speak to Dave Alred about my nutrition? No. I'd speak to my nutritionist or a sports scientist.'

In fact, this was exactly what he did. 'I spoke to a guy called Jason Vale, who's known as the 'Juice Master' within the right circles. I saw how vibrant, energetic and healthy he was and I absolutely wanted to model and replicate that.'

'I think one of the most beautiful things about the world of performance psychology and lifestyle at the moment is that there are so many resources and is so much information out there. Fifteen years ago, if I wanted to load up my laptop to find some goalkeeping tips I'd have to manually switch on the internet and plug in the cable, before connecting to AOL a good few minutes later and then waiting another age for the computer to log itself in… In the modern world, there is so much information on the fingertips of young players: it can be a blessing or a curse.' Given the right tools, young players can ensure that it is a positive addition to their abilities more often than not.

'It might be that you breakdown every area of the game, your lifestyle and your position in which you could improve. Then you've got to find tailored, evidence-based and powerful programmes or strategies for each that you could begin to integrate within your lifestyle.'

I ask Rich about the example of wanting to increase your speed, as a winger: what would he recommend in this scenario? 'I'd suggest that you find yourself a speed programme put together by a top sprinter, with some prominent and credible reviews. You could block off 10 minutes every day that you would dedicate to undertaking and committing fully to this process over the next six weeks. It's almost worthless, in my opinion, if these programmes aren't objectified, though: you have to do something at the very start and at the very end. You may well improve with just an ad-hoc intervention, but you'll see the biggest results - and be able to measure what has been successful and what hasn't - if you can start the programme with a test, finish the programme with a test and then analyse your improvements from there. It helps you gauge where you're at, massively, as well as giving you a heightened level of awareness as to the strengths in your position and what you could possibly do to improve.'

There are literally thousands of appropriate examples for ways that people could improve, but it all comes down to be able to think creatively and 'inside the box', as to what you experience on a match-day and the mechanisms that you can put in place to improve that. This, for Rich, and all those at the top reaches of professional football, is key: what can we do to improve the elements of our game, and how can we ensure the best results by ensuring that this process is as match-realistic as possible? Because, when it comes down to the line, practice doesn't make perfect. It makes permanent. If that permanent practice has been the wrong technique because you haven't been consulting experts, it's easy to see where issues could arise.

ACTION PLAN

There are many margins that you might seek to improve on the football pitch, but the knowledge of how to undertake this betterment is one of the most crucial skills. We've outlined a basic plan below, that you might choose to adjust or alter for yourself.

1) Identify the area that requires improvement

2) Set a goal as to how much and in what way you want to develop it

3) Complete research online as to existing experts in the field, and also websites with useful advice

4) Reach out to these experts and start to collect some of the advice

5) With your new knowledge, put together a training programme to improve the skill

6) Test yourself (if possible) on the first week of the programme

7) Reflect after each session on your own personal performance and how you might improve next time

8) Complete another test at the end of the programme and measure your improvements!

Now, it's important to remember that this is just a very skeleton-like outline: there is much more that needs to be included, but that will be specific to each individual. Hopefully now you can start to think about what you might want to improve in the way you play and how you're going to go about that.

10
PREHABILITATION

With sports scientists involved with professional football clubs from the very early foundation phases, and an awful lot of cash being invested towards preparing physically stable players, it'd be naïve to think that having a strong foundation of strength, range of motion and coordination isn't going to help you in modern football. Especially as we now start to see the hyper-inflation of player transfer fees towards extortionate prices: who's going to be willing to risk their big bucks on an 'injury-prone' signing? Rich agrees, and we discuss the kind of actions that young players - and parents - can take to giving themselves the best chance of an injury-free career.

'I think that you can start to think about preventative measures very early on. There are many lessons to be learned from other topics that we've discussed, because it's all about building a base and then becoming an expert from that. For me, it's about the general foundation of movement patterns and biomechanics, before you then specialise on those extra couple of inches of leap or lateral movement.'

'As a young player, I was a great example of someone who really didn't understand this. I spent a lot of time as an 18-year-old on a basketball-specific plyometrics training programme. Initially, this gave me incredible spring. I added eight or nine inches to my vertical spring, and I can still remember now how powerful I was in the goal that season. I felt physically great, got the England call-up and was generating a lot of positive headlines because of the type of game that I played.'

The problem was, though, that Rich had never built the base, or structure, from which to make these gains. 'I went from doing very little in the way of weight-training or gym work to a very high-intensity schedule, and just expected to be able to specialise on very particular aspects of my game. Over time, I got found out and broke down. My knee went, totally, and then I had numerous issues with my groins as well. A large part of that, if not all, was because I never built the base of strength and core stability in the first place.'

In this case, you might be thinking, what kind of activities will contribute to 'generalised movement patterns' or 'fundamentals' of the game? The answer, simply put, is a variety of different sports in different contexts and with different objectives. 'As a youngster, there's so much value in playing a number of sports. For goalkeepers, it might be something like tennis (for lateral movement) or basketball (for spring and hand-eye coordination), whilst outfield players may be particularly primed towards rugby (an alternative invasion game) or even athletics (from a fitness perspective). What many people don't realise is the generalised movement patterns and motor solutions that this builds up for young players, and gives them such wide foundations that they can go on to specialise with further down the line.'

The disproportionate success of American goalkeepers compared to outfield players is often attributed to the fact that so many youngsters across the pond play a large number of sports with hand-eye coordination and great transfer to goalkeeping (such as basketball, baseball and American football) - this is a great example of how building a wide base of physical capabilities and movement patterns can support players further down the line. Furthermore, a number of footballers have spoken about the influence that martial arts such as Tai Chi and Jiu Jitsu have had on their career at an early age, which Rich cites as another great tool to improving and understanding movement especially. 'If we're talking about how you can understand your own movement and coordination within that, I think that martial arts is a perfect complement to many other sports. It really trains you to think about the way you move, anticipate and predict based on your opponent and requires huge levels of kinaesthesia in order to achieve success.'

Looking at a senior level, and a lot of clubs now have invested heavily in programmes similar to yoga and pilates. 'Being able to control and balance the body is vital, especially if there may usually be an imbalance due to the one-footed nature of the football game that we play. Clubs are doing everything they can now to educate and prepare players in this regard, and understandably so.'

And Rich has regrets over his early scepticism of these programmes, which he looks back on now and assesses how he could've responded differently. 'I wish I'd taken yoga more seriously when I was younger. I remember arriving at Blackburn and Brad Friedel gave me a book about men's yoga; I just took it off him and politely laughed him off. Looking back at the incredibly elongated and sustained career that he's had (still going strong at 42, without an ache or pain in the world), I wish I'd heeded his advice that was along the lines of "Rich - you need to read this… It'll change your footballing career, seriously!".'

At the time, Rich knew little about how correct Brad may have been. A number of years later, though, having retired in his early 30s and with a number of injuries still returning from the game, Rich remarks that half an hour a day back then could've had a potentially massive impact in elongating and revitalising his personal career.

It is clear that the importance of building a strong base early on, then, must not be overlooked or neglected, for the risks are far greater than any potential benefit of leaving it to chance.

11
GOAL SETTING

Students going through the school system at present will likely be inundated with personal and academic targets. The same for those in the academy setup. In 2017, there's a great realisation of the importance of goals and the amount of focus and motivation that they can bring to an athlete. However, the biggest value comes when a player can take the initiative to set their own goals, on their own terms and around the matters that are most important to them. It could well be the difference between following through with the lifestyle restructures we've already spoken about, or falling by the wayside and dropping out halfway through the process.

Most importantly, in Rich's opinion, is the continued setting of goals throughout your performance and journey as a player: as soon as one is completed, the next must be on its way.

'This is probably one of the criticisms that I have of myself from the game: I didn't achieve consistent excellence for a long enough period of time. It's much easier to look at in hindsight, but I think that I set myself a lot of goals around earning contracts and playing in big games. These are fine targets in themselves, but I don't think that I understood that, as soon as goals had been achieved, I should be setting new goals and always searching to develop myself as a player.'

And, beyond that, the bigger picture context of the goals is also imperative to success. 'There needs to be a succession of goals. It might be that you have an end goal that seems a long way away, such as being a Premier League player, and this provides the perfect opportunity for having continuous goals, because you can break down the process into stepping stones and manageable objectives. Weekly goals. Daily goals. Hourly goals. How many achievable steps can you break a goal down to? It'll really help you understand exactly what is required to succeed and how you can achieve that.'

'It'd be wrong to say that one shouldn't enjoy achieving a goal', Rich points out, 'but you certainly have to heed caution around resting on your laurels.'

An issue that is more commonplace in England more than other countries, largely because of the amount of money invested in the game through ownership and broadcasting deals, is that there are a large number of young players who have earned themselves a massive pay cheque at a very young age. There aren't many leagues similar to the Premier League, where there are 18-year-olds on £40,000 or £50,000 a week without having kicked a football in a competitive match. Rich applies these scenarios to the element of goal setting and motivation. 'They lose that little bit of hunger that they used to have in their younger years and that's a trait that's very difficult to artificially replicate. Of course, if you take 99% of human beings and give them a huge lump of cash, it's going to have an impact on their motivations and desires.'

'For the players, it's about having the maturity and desire to look above the money bags and continue trying to perform for the joy and happiness that it undoubtedly brings. Your goals must be set around this, because they are the only metric that will keep you accountable for your own success and ensure that you take on board every opportunity to achieve and reach them.'

It's vital that you use your goals as a tool for remaining grounded and invested in your foreseeable progress, whether that be recovering from an injury, winning a World Cup or breaking the way into the first team as an U18. It's about setting new goals, every day, that will get you excited and help you move up to the next level: the second you think you've 'made it' to the top level is the second that danger begins to engulf your pathway and the skies above you darken…

ACTION PLAN

In most organisations, we will often hear about 'SMART' targets for success in a given activity. Whilst these are undoubtedly important, they often don't appreciate the 'bigger picture' of what you might be dreaming to achieve. Therefore, we're going to propose a two-part system, with 'SMART' targets as your outcome-based stepping stones on the way to a 'DUMB' goal. Let me explain:

Dangerously - Unattainable - Monstrously - Big

This one 'DUMB' goal might be to play in the Premier League. It might be to make a career out of professional football. It might be to represent your country. Either way, it is certainly not the 'realistic' or 'time-specific' goal that a 'SMART' target might represent. However, in order to reach your DUMB goal, many SMART targets will need to be achieved:

EXAMPLE: 14-year-old footballer

DUMB: Make a career out of professional football

SMART #1: Score 15 goals this season

SMART #2: Be offered a new contract at my current club

SMART #3: Be offered a scholarship at any Category 1/2 academy

SMART #4: Make my professional debut by the age of 20

SMART #5: Play 50 games of football by the age of 23

Each SMART target acts as a stepping stone, and our short-term goals, towards the dream of achieving everything that a 'DUMB' objective entails. It will be crucial that you attribute some process-based goals as well to each SMART target (which you can control, such as 'partake in two extra finishing sessions a week') in order to make this journey more achievable.

SECTION #3
SUSTAINED PERFORMANCE

12
BOUNCING BACK

Every professional player, no matter what level they played at, understands the feeling where everything seems as though it's going wrong. You somehow lose 1-0 to a shinned, deflected, back-spinning own goal from outside the box, the referee misses what you believe to be a blatant penalty and all of a sudden the barrage of support you've been used to for so many years has become a carnivorous pack of criticisers, baying for blood through the first scapegoat that they can find. Rich has experienced it just as much as others, but speaks free of emotion and with a different perspective about how we should view it.

'Bad form is an interesting one for me. The reality is that we often misjudge negative performances, or at least the context behind them, based on the fact that we've just lost a game of football.'

'The advice that I wish that I'd given myself is to be very careful what you link bad form to. Everyone talks very happily about 'learning lessons' from failure, but it's a bit more complicated than that: it's about learning the right lessons. To assign bad form to something specific that might have no causal relationship could be very negative for you in the way that you play and where you're focussing your energy. You can't go off-track by putting blame on something that could be totally unrelated, and using that purely as a release for your frustrations and anger.'

It can be difficult to work out what the actual cause of bad performance might be (as opposed to attributing it to random areas of the game that might have only had a minute impact on the result), and that becomes even harder with an appreciation that the 'bad form' might not even exist.

'The other side of it is actually the understanding of whether the bad form existed in the first place. As a goalkeeper, I suppose we notice this a lot more than other positions. For instance, a good example of this is a guy that we look after who played a string of games last season, where his team were consistently losing and not finding results. Naturally, he beat himself up about it and didn't really know what he could do to improve moving forwards. We had a look at the stats and the video footage, and came to a really simple but significant conclusion: there was nothing wrong with the goalkeeping at all (in fact, he was conceding less than a goal a game on average): the problem was the fact that the side weren't scoring any goals at the other end of the pitch. The general vibe around the ground would've been a negative one, and that can then manifest itself towards the way in which you view your performance, finding mistakes where there aren't any and generally diminishing your confidence.' For me, the last sentence within this short example from Rich is the most significant to players at any stage of their development: you have to be able to remove the environment from which you are working in, in order to objectively assess your performance.

Another strategy, also around detaching yourself from the emotions of the game, comes in the way of an individual coach. 'Having an individual coach is always a very powerful mechanism for a player when it comes to understanding their form objectively. They can look at and assess your game without having to worry about the other 10 players on the field, and this can mean that their analysis is much more performance-centred and not unduly swayed by a negative result.'

Once the game's over, as well, the ability to watch back objectively can be incredibly useful, because it can be very easy to generalise the term bad form. 'If you make two mistakes over the course of 90 minutes, does that make the game a 5/10? Well, those two mistakes might have led to goals. On another day, those two mistakes didn't lead to goals and you win 5-0. Does that make it an inherently better game?' There are so many variables that may have influenced your performance before the match, such as sleep patterns, training performance or a bit of self-doubt, and it can be massively overwhelming to try and deal with all of these when you're analysing your bad form, and that's why a specific coach - or neutral spectator - can be vital in helping you to brush aside the red herrings from the margins that will improve your performance.

Rich has seen players being caught up by the irrelevant details all too much in the past, with some rather strange excuses amongst them. 'I've seen some mad players over the year blame their performance on having eaten broccoli the night before, and this is an example of getting far too caught up in the margins whilst possibly neglecting the gaping areas of your performance that might need improving first - it's about not wasting valuable energy on explanations which may or may not exist.'

To conclude, though, and far beyond the essence of analysis, Rich speaks about the ability to turn around bad form as one that is a fight or flight mechanism, a term some of you may be familiar with already.

'In times of bad performance, when the cards are stacked against you, how do you respond? It's all about having a positive attitude to use this as a driving force, and the mindset to pick yourself back up and perform excellently once more. For me, there's no right or wrong motivations: just different intensities. As long as you can harness the full power of that motivation, whether it be towards performance, pressure, or merely reversing the vibes of the last two defeats, it's a worthy intent for me. I've had experiences where players have completely turned around situations where they were being booed and heckled by fans, were out of touch and really not enjoying their time at a club. If you can figure this out, and how you deal with it, then you become almost invincible, because you'll always have that technique and mechanism for bouncing back from failure with strength, which you can replicate whenever it's required.'

13

ANALYSIS

In the era of TV pundits, online footballing bloggers and copious tactical handbooks on the game of football, many believe that 'analysis' is little more than something reserved for the top dogs in sport, with the backroom staff and structures in place to interrogate every inch of their performance on the pitch. I ask Rich what he understands by analysis, before we delve into how players who might not be blessed with Premier League resources can ensure that they're still using one of the greatest tools for technical improvement and psychological stability.

'Having someone on your side, who wants the best for you and will fight your corner where necessary is a god send in the world of football', explains Rich. 'It's a person who must be invested in your continued improvement, and dedicated to helping you perform, but also someone who has the ability to communicate your strengths and shortcomings effectively and with a great deal of knowledge and inspiration.' If you can have someone in your network who can work with and appreciate this, then you don't really need to worry about analysis too much: just focus on the areas that we discussed during 'bad form' and you should be set to use the opinions from those around you in the best possible light.

The situation for the majority, though, is not so rosy. For a young or non-league player, who might not have the same tools in the way of dedicated support staff, a really crucial piece of advice from Rich is to obtain video footage of their matches. 'In the world we live in, technology is so readily available, and all players should take the opportunity to review themselves objectively after the game has been played. It's always interesting how watching yourself back often doesn't look as it felt on the football pitch, and this can be a very different - but fruitful - feedback mechanism for developing your own performance. You're seeing what somebody else sees; sometimes this can be the first time that a coaching point really clicks and you understand what is required to improve.'

I ask Rich whether he believes that the individual player themselves should undertake the analysis, or if they should speak to the staff around them to support the process. 'Certainly, it's an area where you have to be careful, because the opinions of those around you will often contradict each other and can leave you feeling confused and with little idea of what needs to come next. Understanding which opinions will drive you forward, and which won't, is also a great strength to have. You must take each opinion with a filter that can help you to assess whether it will be beneficial or detrimental, and then deal with it as necessary from there.'

'You can never, ever, make 100% of the population, 100% happy with you, 100% of the time. It's just not possible and isn't close to being so. There are people out there who are always going to say you're useless, regardless of how much those opinions might actually mean. The important message is being able to understand and appreciate when to heed the words of caution and wisdom from those around you, without succumbing to the pitfalls of constant and irrelevant criticism. As a fundamental, though, your analysis should always come back and revolve around you and your own views on performance.'

Video analysis is an excellent tool, but there are many other ways to measure and analyse your performance as well. 'I'm a massive advocate of objective markers', says Rich. 'Often, I'll advise that my goalkeepers focus on a specific area of their play - and outfielders could do the same - before going away to undertake really concentrated and specific work towards this. It could be a technical skill such as the ability to make a pass or strike the ball, whilst it's possible that you might look at something more match-realistic in the sense of scoring one-on-ones or getting on the end of a cross.'

'I'll then suggest that they come back to the programme six weeks or so later, and reassess themselves: are they higher or lower? If they're higher, then they can start to look for another programme or margin that might need improvement. If they're lower, or at a similar level, then they have to reflect on what might have held them back over the past few weeks and design a solution to ensure that it doesn't hold them down long-term. It might not be a rigid way to analyse a given performance, but it can absolutely help you to analyse and develop over a longer period of time.'

14
CONFIDENCE

Throughout his career, confidence was maybe the one element of his game that eluded Rich most, which is even more surprising given his entrepreneurial and risk-taking background away from football. 'I was always a lot quieter than the other goalkeepers, which made me question quite often whether I was as good as them or not. It was only when I was 15 or 16, and had a call-up to the England squad, that I started to feel a greater level of self-assurance in my performance.'

This wasn't the only positive event that helped to build Rich's confidence, though, as the media and fan base were building a positive (for once) mental image for his career as well. 'Even when I was young, there were rumours going around the club that I'd already signed a professional contract (totally false at the time); to know that people saw you in that light was a big belief- and confidence-builder. I thought that if everyone around me could see it and thought I was going to be successful, then it must be true.' He's quick to recognise, at the same time, that he still hadn't achieved an internal foundation of self-efficacy, which maybe was seen through the young years of his career: his only belief and confidence was from the external environment by which he was surrounded.

Moving onto how this intrinsic belief and motivation can be built, and Rich has ideas aplenty that he utilises often with his agency work. 'There are a load of key factors that can help someone's intrinsic motivation, and I truly believe that young goalkeepers should be dealing with and tackling these kinds of thoughts as soon as they're mature enough.'

'Affirmations are a massive way to build confidence from within', Rich begins. 'Telling yourself what you want to believe and subsequently taking action to try and achieve that is incredibly powerful as a technique for increasing confidence. You can embed this into your subconscious with great levels of effectiveness using a neuro-linguistic programming technique called 'anchoring'.'

It may sound a complex topic, full of complex language, without a doubt, but the basic principles are quite straightforward and easily transferable to players of any age. 'You have to think about and imagine your game in great depth and detail, analysing the picture of the different scenarios that you might possibly face (trying to beat a defender 1v1, dealing with a corner or making a 50-yard pass).'

'Then, you must absorb and assimilate every fine detail from that environment. We're talking about everything from the standing foot of the shooter, to the make of the ball, to the raucous fans who may be stood behind the goal. Using these pictures, you can generate strong and positive feelings of confidence, belief and euphoria, that you can then start to associate alongside the different scenarios. It will help you to rig your mind to positive sensations during the game of football, and can work wonders for being internally driven to believing that you can succeed.'

'Of course, this isn't the easiest thing to teach to a 10- or 12-year-old, but it is something that can be coached and will likely become second-nature if they've been exposed to it from a young age', Rich replies, when I question the sort of age at which he believes this is best started at.

'The quicker you can start to dictate your own state is the quicker that you will be able to command the long-term nature of your career, and the joy that you have through that as well. If you're a nervous and unstable player, you might get away with one or two bad games, or even seasons if you're still performing technically, but over time you're either going to lose the love for the game or it's going to harm you emotionally.'

ACTION PLAN

We mention affirmations in this section of the book, but without going into too much detail about how you can use them to support your game. Here's all the information that you need to know.

Definition

A self-affirmation is the expressing of a positive attitude towards yourself, generally in the form of a positive statement that you repeat daily. It helps in competitive and performance situations where players believe they can win by being positive and focussing on goals.

(Adapted from psychologydictionary.org)

Strategy

1) List negative affirmations

To start, whilst it might seem counter-intuitive, make a list of all the negative ways in which you see yourself on the football pitch at present. It could be using words such as 'timid', 'lazy' or 'unskilled', but the idea is that you can really understand which parts of your game you have the least confidence about so that you can combat them moving forwards.

2) Create positives from these

Then, take every negative affirmation that you've made on the list and replace this with its positive counterpart. It could be that 'timid' becomes 'confident', 'lazy' to 'energetic' or 'unskilled' to 'talented' - it's absolutely up to you. In order to further build these ideas, you might want to consult a thesaurus to use more powerful words and have a greater impact on your game.

3) Recite your new affirmations

With your new bank of positive and confidence-building adjectives in hand, now is your chance to associate these with the football pitch. Before every training session, every morning and every evening, spend five minutes saying these affirmations out loud, whilst visualising your improved performance on the pitch. The more that you can truly 'believe' what you are saying, and that it will transfer into your matches, the better.

4) Get a coach to repeat affirmations

Where possible, the more people that are helping you to believe your affirmations and use them on the pitch, the better. Telling your coach about a couple of the trigger words that you've been working on might help them to refocus you on the pitch, whilst they can also work on integrating the positive affirmations within good moments at training and during matches. It's a joint effort.

15
PRESSURE

In the world of sports psychology, the word pressure is discussed in many different concepts and contexts, with a variety of theories outlining how we deal with it and the role it plays within our sporting career. Some will believe that our ability to process and deal with pressure is as a result of innate qualities and characteristics, whereas others suggest that these skills will emerge from the situations and environments that we are exposed to during our development. The one message, however, is clear: pressure has the ability to make or break a young player's career. It is an ever-present quirk of the world of sport, but one that Rich believes we can be in total control of, with the right preparation, training and mindset. 'The idea of pressure really fascinates me. Without going into too much detail about the underlying psychological theories, something that I learned and resonated with very early on in my career was the idea that pressure isn't always a conscious mechanism. We all have individual factors within the way that we react to pressure, likely as a combination of our genetic and environmental influences through the years. At the start of my career, I certainly found myself in the nervous camp when it came to pressure: I got very nervous and anxious during games of football and felt the weight of expectation on my shoulders.'

However, Rich suggests that the pressure was his to accept or reject over time. 'It is an internal element that is created through the way in which we perceive any given situation. If you allow the social inhibition of playing infront of 50,000 people to rise to the forefront of your mind, then you will be anchored by the pressure and expectation of that situation. It's the way we see this pressure as a threat to our ego or reputation, and this might be heightened by the big matches such as a debut or cup final.'

An interesting concept, and obviously one that young players will want to understand how to combat and improve within their game. 'The biggest facet for improving this is, at first, understanding the way in which you are affected and the trigger, or root cause, of the issue: it's only from this point that one can begin to mould and manipulate their mind to work with (as opposed to against) the psychological pressures. When you have the knowledge that pressure can only impact you intrinsically, then you will start to be able to build mechanisms and behaviours to deal with, negate and transform the pressure you're feeling into positive energy.'

'It can be really impactful, because you start to generate the idea that even the worst case scenario is not going to break you: if you make a really bad error and cost your team a goal, you will still come back for the next shot and have the power to change your mindset. I think a lot of the time we can make conscious decisions about the way we feel, if we have the levels of awareness to allow that.'

'You can choose to go home from the game incredibly down and lacking confidence, and have a cry if you want, or you can decide to take a very different perspective and entertain a mindset of continual development, taking the positives from the situation and using it to better yourself in the future: it can become a never-ending cycle, purely because of the way in which you interpret your performance.'

Clearly, this is not an overnight revelation, and I put this point to Rich: 'it takes a bit of time, education and training to reach the point where you have these levels of self-awareness and opportunity to mould your conscious and unconscious mind, but the ability to be able to dictate and adapt your mindset based on any situation is a crucial skill if you want to give yourself the best chance of coping psychologically with the highest levels of football.'

He follows this with an example of a goalkeeper that is often mentioned as having a particularly exceptional approach towards pressure, that we also speak to personally later in the book. 'Ben Foster would always be so intrinsically wired to enjoy big games of football; it was incredible. I remember being in the quarter-final of The FA Cup against Plymouth one year. The conditions were nothing short of horrific. Grey and black clouds sealed the sky above our heads, the rain was lashing down and there was such a strong wind that it could be difficult to hear one another in conversation from just a few metres. I've never seen someone quite so excited as Ben was for that warm up. It was probably quite a polar opposite to me, because I spent a lot of my time just trying to 'get through' a fixture, and ensure that I didn't make a costly error for the team. Ben's outlook, on the other hand, was that he couldn't wait to get out on the pitch and be the hero. His approach started to ignite a lightbulb within my brain, and certainly struck a chord with me, because he was so willing and eager to embrace challenge that it gave an almost imperious and unbeatable persona to his character on the pitch.'

But it wasn't just his pre-game characteristics that impressed Rich. 'Even the way in which he would react to poor fortunes impressed me. He was the goalkeeper who was victim to Paul Robinson's goal a few years back (the former England 'keeper scored from a free kick just outside his own area), and I would've been so mortified that I wanted the ground to swallow me up if I'd been on the receiving end of such an error. So was Ben's character, though, that he came in after the final whistle and was laughing: he thought it was hilarious! He trained as hard as anyone during the week, but come match-day there was an almost care-free attitude about the way he played. If he had a blinder, he had a blinder. If he conceded a howler, he conceded a howler. Either way, he knew that he would go back to his family, enjoy his evening and that his life in professional football would continue - he'd have other opportunities to prove himself moving forwards.'

In conclusion, then, I ask Rich what creates this ability to take total control over the pressure in a young footballer's game, and what Ben had tapped into so well to achieve great levels of psychological success. 'It comes back to that mindset and the way in which he approached and dealt with the pressure he was served. Some of it will be innate and how he was genetically constructed, but I think a massive part of it can be, and certainly was for Ben, picked up and honed environmentally, if the focus and attitude is there to make it count.' Starting to put yourself in positions of pressure as a player, and looking at psychological techniques to deal with this, can be imperative to improving your ability to perform under pressure. It is almost as if enjoying the mistakes, sometimes, and understanding that they're a mechanism to improve moving forwards, will help you deal with pressure best in the long-run.

ACTION PLAN

Pressure is a topic that has featured very regularly throughout the book, in different areas and through different parts of the game of football. Having the tools in the locker to deal with pressure at a high level will be crucial to any potential success, and here are just a couple of skills that you can utilise.

Reframing pressure

Do you see pressure as a negative or a positive? Is it something that will help you to perform and be the hero or something that will throw you under the bus? Why do you have this view of pressure? The first step to dealing with pressure is to understand how you can reframe it to support your game in a more positive way. Instead of believing that pressure is going to hold you back or hinder your performance, spend some time thinking about, studying and admiring athletes who really excel under pressure, and see if you can start to emulate some of their mindsets or characteristics on the pitch. You can choose exactly how you feel in any given moment, so it's all about trying to gear it towards being excited and confident.

Keeping habit

Pre-match, it is easy to panic. Have I done everything I need to do? Have I prepared in the best possible manner? What if I've forgotten something?! Being able to keep to a set, habitual routine will help you massively in your ability to reduce the nerves that any pressure gives you. Some suggest keeping a checklist of everything that you need to do pre-match, whilst another strategy is to create a pre-match routine with your coach or psychologist that you can follow regardless of the situation.

Mental rehearsal

Linking in with our first point, mental rehearsal is a skill used by a large number of world-class athletes. Essentially, it's taking some time away from everything else to close your eyes and picture what success looks like on the pitch. Imagine yourself scoring a 35-yard wonder goal, tipping a venomous free-kick over the crossbar or making a crunching tackle on the oppositions centre-forward. Make sure that these experiences are positive; they will form the energy that you feel towards the game when it begins.

These are three very simple but very powerful ways in which you can start to deal with pressure in your own life and game. There are many more strategies (such as mindfulness and self-talk) that your club psychologist might be able to support you with.

16
GIANTS VS UNDERDOGS

David vs Goliath. The giant vs the underdog. Whether it be Blythe Spartans in The FA Cup or Leicester City in the Premier League, there is a natural feeling that something special is in the air when those who were given no hope overcome great odds to achieve victory. The science behind this phenomenon, though, is one that lacks any real clarity. In the world of professional football, the sensations are immensely powerful.

'A really interesting feeling that a lot of people assume when they are the underdogs is one of liberation and freedom. It's probably just a feature of our culture and society, but we all want the underdog to be successful. I don't know if anyone has ever questioned why exactly that is, because it doesn't make a great deal of logical sense, but it does allow us to remove the fear or worry about performance when we are the underdogs up against a much bigger team. You were never expected to win, nor to even compete, so imagine the jubilation when you end up winning the fixture.'

Over his years in the game, Rich has had a number of experiences where he felt that his side weren't expected to win. 'Beating Everton in the cup with Brentford was certainly up there as one of those events. I saved a penalty, had a really good evening in the goal and, when I look back, I can't remember too many times where I'm happier with my performance than I was that night. This was a game from which very little was expected from Rich and his teammates, and it is often these fixtures where the best performances are realised.

'The amount of euphoria that seemed to follow that was incredible: they even started to create some memorabilia from the tie, and I think my face appeared on a couple of mugs', Rich recalls, jokingly.

'I look back now, and the game itself was a little bit strange. I had no nerves in anticipation of the match, just a strange feeling that - regardless of the result - we would be comforted and almost held as champions anyway.' Without a doubt, it's the kind of feeling that many footballers -

or any sports people - have experienced from time to time, and it can pay massive dividends on the football field.

'On the flip side, though', Rich reminds me, 'being the favourite to win a match can often be one of the most difficult positions in football. Not only are you expected to give your all, but there's a unanimous expectation that your all will be enough to win the game very comfortably, and by a margin of four, five or six goals. The pressure is to be expected, but is another cultural thing.'

Some players will struggle with this weight on their shoulders, without the tools to deal with the issues effectively. Others will thrive on the pressure and love the feeling of knowing that they have to win, or their necks will be on the line. Rich and I discuss why, and how, these feelings come about and, of course, how to manipulate them in your favour.

'Both of these scenarios comes back to many aspects of this book: it's how you perceive what's around you that really counts. Being the underdog, or the giant, has no net effect on your performance (it's irrelevant on paper) because you've still got the same opportunities to go out onto that pitch and play to the absolute best of your abilities.'

Rich accepts, on the other hand, that when match-day arrives the situation can be somewhat different. 'As usual, the theory in this regard is much easier than its execution, and I don't think there's anyone who would put the blame on a 'giant' for struggling during a game.' Being able to empathise with this expectation is one of the many qualities that Rich used when building up techniques to deal with these emotions for his young players.

'An interesting tool to try and combat these feelings, especially from the perspective of working 'with' as opposed to 'against' feelings, is to undertake some coaching to breed the feelings of being an underdog regardless of whether you are favourites or not.'

'Let me explain', Rich says.

'If you suddenly feel like you've got the freedom of the underdog, and you step across that white line knowing that you can't lose, then your performance is going to be significantly increased because of it. Imagine if you could harness that feeling for every game. Why can't you feel that way before every game, even those that you're expected to win? If that freedom allows you to express yourself a little bit more, then why would you try and starve yourself from those opportunities? At the same time, if you feel as though you're motivated and most inspired by feeling like the favourite, that you're going to powerhouse the opposition into submission, then recreate those feelings before the game and try to maximise on your emotions from there.'

There's no right or wrong answer within any of this, because it's all about gearing and fine-tuning your mind to what works best for you as an individual: everyone has a very unique optimum performance level. However, with the amount of impact that your psychological state can have on the way you perform, Rich is sure that there is a massive benefit to coaching, and training your mind to believe it's the underdog or favourite, dependent on what works best for you. Give it a go, and let the results speak for themselves.

17
CULTURE OF EXCELLENCE

In today's society, the topic of 'organisational psychology' is growing rapidly. Basically, it is the idea of understanding and moulding the way in which different parts of a group or organisation work together, in order to create the best possible performance outcomes and chances of success. Excellence is a huge part of this, and the mindset to achieve it is one that Rich has great experience in harnessing.

'If you go into the gym at a football club, there might be a piece of rubbish on the floor. That individual, isolated piece of rubbish doesn't mean - or change - anything within the chances of success for the team. However, this is where the idea that things can always improve comes in. Very soon, that one piece of litter could become two or three, because others start to think that it's acceptable to leave their rubbish on the floor, and all of a sudden a whole organisation is infested with a potentially performance-related issue, purely because of something that could've been nipped in the bud in its very early stages.'

'It's similar to going into a kitchen that's in a bit of a state: if you were to eat your food in a dirty kitchen, there's going to be much more of a tendency just to leave the plate on the side without washing it up, compared to going into a spotless kitchen, where there's going to be a totally different feeling because you're going to want to clean your plate.

You wouldn't dare leave it dirty on the side.'

'Your mind works in very much the same way', Rich explains, brining the subject back to your individual improvement. 'If you're OK to let things slip a little bit, it can be very difficult to prevent them slipping a lot. Whether it be a late night, eating badly before a training session or the entrance of alcohol into your life, all your focus starts to move away from football without you even recognising it.'

The spiral will continue, and be harder and harder to stem. Before long, you will start to lose real percentages from your game that could have a massive impact on your future potential. Everyone understands that to hold yourself to the highest levels of performance on a regular basis is no easy task, but Rich uses a number of tactics with his footballers to try and improve the way in which they search for their own levels of excellence.

'I think a lot of the strategy behind this comes down to the awareness of the moments that you do allow yourself to slip. It's very easy to point out to your friend when they slip, or when they make a mistake; it is an awful lot harder to do that within your own performance and lifestyle.'

'A large part on the way to preventing these small hiccups from upsetting a larger trend within your game is through taking a great deal of responsibility and honesty over your behaviour. You shouldn't try to excuse or justify poor decisions: it's the difference between merely claiming "Ah, well... I worked really hard today so I deserved that burger before training" and actually fronting up to the slip that you've had, understanding that it's definitely a negative towards your goals and thinking about how you can discourage this type of action in the future.'

If awareness is the first step, then you may already be aware that 'perfect excellence' isn't a realistic target for you (in fact, many would say it is impossible to achieve). Rich talks about how you can manage the less positive aspects of your lifestyle, without allowing them to engulf your overall development.

'When I work with many of our footballers, it isn't always about trying to hit perfection, at least not to begin with. We might devise a strategy that looks at all the meals they have in a particular week, and then say that one of those meals can be a 'cheat meal'. If they can get the other 20 spot on, then the damage limitation of taking one meal off the plan is better than the potential spiral that might follow if they can't stick to what's expected of them. It's having that mentality where you set yourself to a higher standard, but also understanding that you shouldn't expect the absolute impossible from yourself.'

Our conversation then moves forward to a discussion as to how players can measure themselves in this regard, and the kind of actions they can take to build a strong mindset, or indeed culture, of excellence.

'The most important aspect, for me, is to understand the learning process behind how we learn and make changes to our lifestyle.' The below model summarises Rich's thoughts perfectly:

Unconsciously incompetent - This is the start of the process: you have no knowledge of what you're doing wrong, we'll use the example of learning to drive. This is where you have no idea of what you're doing, and so don't understand why the car stalls after you switch on the engine and try to drive away.

Consciously incompetent - Here, you are made aware that what you're doing is wrong, generally as a result of someone educating you, some new information that comes out or any other means of recognition (it might be a club nutrition workshop, or a Biology lesson at school). In our example, this is where you start your driving lessons and have learned you need to bring up the clutch to biting point before you drive off.

Consciously competent - The first stage in which real changes will occur, this is where you intentionally act in a different way in order to avoid whatever the negative behaviour might be. It might take a lot of effort, and you might not always get it right, but you're trying and having success with changes in the way you act. In this scenario, it's the point at which you can successfully drive off, providing that you think consciously about lifting your foot slightly every time that you want to start moving.

Unconsciously competent - Where everything comes together, this is where naturally you are behaving in the desired manner, without any conscious thought-processing. You will just naturally drive away, without even thinking about the movement of your feet, and rarely have a problem with this skill. It is the stage at which you become what we call 'autonomous' in a given field, and will allow you to move on to the next area of lifestyle improvement that you seek to make.

18
CULTURE OF EXCELLENCE (SQUAD)

A culture of excellence isn't just reserved to individuals. Beyond that, a culture of excellence can be created throughout an entire team, squad or organisation. Once you've mastered, or at least started to get to grips with, how you can design your life towards achieving excellence, there is a great opportunity to have an impact on your team.

'The next stage of this is to have the awareness of those around you as well. If you're living to high standards (and enjoying the success within that), it is vital that this isn't hindered through the poor actions of your teammates: you have to pick them up on their negative behaviours.'

I ask Rich about how a player can influence this in a constructive manner. 'There are so many ways that your teammates might find themselves slipping, whether that be one of the examples that we've already looked at (a piece of rubbish on the floor, poor sleep and bad eating habits) or even something training-related such as not warming up to the best of their ability, or skipping the daily yoga programme. It's all of these areas that, once you're fully responsible for yourself, you need to start helping your teammates with if you want the best chance of success as a team.'

It's not about one individual margin slipping for one individual player;

it's about the potential repercussions and spiral that could happen as a result of this, as we've already discussed.

'The All Blacks are a perfect example of where there is such an abrupt honesty within the whole culture, and I think that's gone a long way to creating the success that they've achieved in the game. In the normal world, whenever you're given a piece of criticism or told to do something, the natural reaction is to become defensive, shield yourself away from it and be quite rigid as to how you might adjust your behaviour. On the other hand, within this New Zealand environment, there was just a total acceptance of any piece of advice that was given.'

'It's not to say that the opinion is always correct', points out Rich, 'but the players will always welcome the information to try and improve and enhance their performance further in the future.'

Within your own teams, Rich has a number of ideas as to how you can support that process of stepping up and being honest where necessary. It takes a great deal of character, clearly, but is vital if you want to deliver the best possible and most consistent performances as a team.

'As opposed to watching another player drop that piece of litter on the floor, and then telling another teammate behind their back, why not just say to the player's face "pick up that piece of litter". You might adjust your tone and chosen words depending on who you're speaking to, but there needs to be that dialogue that this isn't acceptable in the training environment. The same applies to any aspect of training, and it might be something on the field as much as anything else.'

The natural question here will always be around how your teammates might perceive this 'order', if you like: is it going to lose you friends or teammates in the dressing room?

'We speak a lot in football about 'stepping over the white line', and that's massive for me in terms of our character and having this honest approach to speaking to those around us. When you're in 'work mode', then the persona that you take on needs to be one that holds responsibility to its highest regard, and you have to have an agenda to play at your absolute best. Off the pitch, and away from the footballing environment, of course this changes massively and it's fine to be much more relaxed and laid back. If other players aren't willing to appreciate and accept that, then they're not really invested in becoming the best athlete that they can possibly be.'

Again, Rich appreciates that moving into different scenarios and changing rooms can make this task a more difficult ask. It's one thing explaining to the scholars at training that they shouldn't be leaving their empty bottles on the pitch; quite another to tell a seasoned non-leaguer that their off-field actions are preventing the team from progressing.

'I work with a lot of young players, and it can be quite tough to maintain this brutal honesty when you're speaking to someone 12 years your senior. Imagine going into a non-league team and telling the record club goalscorer that he shouldn't be going out getting wasted on a Friday night... It's very difficult!'

'My advice, though, is that you've got to do it. It's your responsibility, as a teammate, to help them and help the team through having the confidence to convey whatever it is about their behaviour that might be unacceptable. Of course, you're not going to scream, shout and give them the hairdryer treatment, but in a team that's striving for excellence, everybody has to be aware of what's acceptable and what's pushing the limit too far.'

At this point, I challenge Rich as to whether it could be of more detriment to a young player than it's worth in performance terms.

'This is the point at which leaders are born. They have to have certain qualities. They're not always the loudest or the strongest, but they will absolutely always have the confidence to exert their responsibility and help those around them to improve their game, through always pushing and seeking for those higher levels of performance.'

It might not be that every player has the authority or audacity to speak out in search of seeking excellence for their team, but those that do are likely to be the players that reach the very top levels of the game: the ones with the mindset, confidence and dedication towards achieving absolute success. It's a sink or swim moment, without a doubt, and it might be that your voice is thanked further down the line, even if it earns you some degree of disrespect in the first place.

19
BALANCE

Even when you're squeezing every margin from your game, and searching tirelessly for those small improvements from which success can be achieved, balance is required. Note, though, that no-one is saying that balance is equal to moderation, but purely that every individual will have a different metric that they should not break from for any sizeable period of time, as Rich explains. 'A really important aspect of balance is the fact that everyone has a different gauge. There's no right or wrong answer in this scenario because everybody is different in the levels of activity that they can consistently sustain.'

'The biggest thing is your self-awareness, which we've mentioned many times. If you're playing 40 hours of football a week, absolutely loving every minute of it and performing out of your skin at the same time, then who am I to tell you that it's too much and you need to cut down to protect yourself psychologically? That would be morally and logically irrational of me. If you're out of balance, though, you'll know it: your fuse will shorten, your energy levels will decrease and you might find that the people around you are less responsive as well. Being in this state, there's not a chance that you're going to train particularly well and reach the levels of performance that you require within a session. It might be that you just need to take a day off, and not focus on football in any way at all.'

'Something that I recommend to the footballers that I work with is to pre-plan their weekly schedule, but also to allow flexibility within that for natural matters that may arise. Often, we use the Sunday evening to give them the chance to predict and plan how many technical, tactical, physical and psychological sessions that they can fit within the coming week. At the end of the week, the players will then have the opportunity to reflect on their week of balance, assess the intensity and tick off however many sessions they managed to participate in.'

'This should be a really positive experience', points out Rich. 'You should feel fulfilled by what you have managed to accomplish. If this is not the case, then we might have to assess the way we're training, and look at whether that balance is currently being achieved: do you need to schedule in more downtime to enjoy and focus on the football when the moment arrives?'

One of the key elements of balance might not actually be the actual percentages between football time and non-football time, but instead focussing on creating positive associations and energy alongside your training and lifestyle. 'I think there's also the difference between playing football because it's your passion (similar to the first example) and playing it because the wage packet coming in every month justifies the boredom (which is where you might find you've lost that balance). I liken it to the common New Year's resolution of joining a gym: it's not done because people are passionate about going to the gym, but out of fear of becoming overweight or being unfit. Therefore, they're in a situation where they're not waking up and looking forward to a work out; they're dreading it. And this breeds negative connotations, strengthening the negative attitude towards going to the gym. These individuals will need something substantial to have any chance of changing these attitudes in the future.'

'It's the same with football: if you feel like you're merely engaging in activity because you have to check a tick box, then you're not going to train and acquit yourself with the same levels of passion and dedication than if you were intrinsically driven to become your best; if you're doing something against your will, you're going to move downhill regardless of how hard you push at it.'

For footballers that undoubtedly find themselves in this rut from time to time, where the proactive strategies that we've already discussed in the book are too late, I ask what players can do to give themselves the best chance of rejuvenation. 'In order to recreate these positive vibes, it can be something as simple as taking a day or two off to relax, wind down and realign your visions towards why it is you're playing football and want to succeed. Being out in nature is important, and many footballers achieve this through playing golf or spending time with the family, because it allows them to totally switch off from the sport and then become excited about the future opportunity to play and improve once more.'

20
PASSION

A lot of the sacrifices that we talk about at times can sound very daunting to a young player. If you mix that in with the actions that you need to take, as well, to reach that level, then it can be very easy to understand just how reluctant or nervous they may feel about the world of professional football. As the saying goes, however, where there's a will, there's a way.

'If it's something that you want to do and are driven to achieving, then it doesn't become a box-ticking exercise; it is something that you look forward to and desire. Trying to fit yoga, pilates, technical work, tactical work, meditation, nutrition plans and more into a day is a very difficult task as it is, and that becomes all the more impossible if you're not enjoying the process or you don't have the desire to achieve the end goal from your sacrifice. It can be like doing the worst job in the world. Your worst and most harrowing nightmare. However, if it is something that you are intrinsically motivated towards, and massively passionate for, then you're going to wake up burning to kindle that desire and get to work with whatever tasks the day may hold for you.'

It seems that every young player starts their journey into the footballing world with great expectations and hopes towards achieving in the professional game, with endless bounds of enthusiasm at every turn in the road. Over the years, this clearly tapers off. Rich's experience of this is as fascinating as it is damning of many aspects of our current system.

'Naturally, a young child will feel the endorphins and the natural high that comes with playing football, as soon as they go down to the park for a kick-about with their parents or friends in their early years. They love kicking the football, scoring a goal and imagining that they're the best footballer in the world.'

'That can die as time goes on. The more criticism you get, the less valued you feel and the less you believe that the people around you are interested in your success, the quicker that the internal passion for the game will wilt: no longer will you want to play the game of football.'

'Significance, and self-fulfilment, is one of our major needs, and suffocating that will likely remove a lot of desire and passion to play from the game in the minds of youngsters.'

There must be something, in this case, that can be done to foster an intrinsic love of the game beyond the early years, and we've already spoken about some of them early in the book.

'Parents have a vital role. They have to understand that, as a child, the balance that they strive for must be so carefully thought out. Every child will need to be exposed to different levels and amounts of football, in different contexts depending on what makes them tick, and making sure that the parents get this aspect right in the early days will play a big part in ensuring that their passion continues. Football, even at the age of 10 or 12 years old, can become - or seem to become - a job. There's so much value in just building the intrinsic love for the game whilst a player is in their infancy, and ensure that they'll want to keep improving and be the best that they can be for many years to come.'

We often talk about players who just 'love to play football' and others who have 'no interest in the game' outside of their job. Often, we are filled with the idea that this was an innate element of that player's personality: they were simply born with a love, or indifference, towards football. The reality is probably quite different. Their feelings towards the game now will most likely be as a result of their earliest footballing experiences, and the positivity and enthusiasm that they've been exposed to throughout this time.

'You can see some players, who are still involved in the game well into their late 30s just have that intrinsic desire and passion for saving the ball, scoring a goal or putting in a crunching challenge. They're not doing it for the money, they don't need that anymore: they're playing because they absolutely love and adore the emotions of being out on the football pitch. It's this kind of attitude that will mean that you're always improving, always moving forward and always drawing the best possible results from your game. I certainly believe that it's something that can be developed, and maybe something we don't think of quite enough in the very organised and structured nature of English sports.'

Moving towards a continued desire to play, and Rich believes that having a purpose in the game holds great value in fuelling the passion of players, especially in the professional context.

'The 'why' is a bit of a cliché in the modern day. There's reason for that, though, because it's an incredibly powerful concept that can motivate individual players and teams massively. Your 'why' for playing football will likely be very unique. It might be your friends, your family, or your reputation, but everyone will have one somewhere at the root of their being and philosophies.'

I ask Rich what he thinks the biggest 'why' is for professional footballers.

'I think that family is a massive one for a lot of players. They know that football is a vehicle for producing a really good living and lifestyle for their partners and kids, and therefore this is one of the main reasons that they strive so much to achieve in the game.'

'I've seen first hand on a large number of occasions that the profound influence having a child can have on a player. As soon as they've got a kid, that's it: they're fighting for that place on the team sheet, so they can get the next big move or wage rise, which means that they'll be able to provide a better standard of living for their children and family. It's not to say that every professional footballer should settle down and have a family, but it's a good example of how a player's passion can increase with a powerful 'why'!'

As a young player, Rich's purpose was along a very different line, but clearly shows that you can be motivated at any age to achieve your dreams.

'It's a story that I probably told in my last book, but something happened when I was 12 years old and plying my trade at Watford. I discovered girls. There was one person in particular that I'd developed a real affection for. In my young mind, the footballers got all the girls, and could pick and choose as they so desired, so I plugged everything into my ability on the football pitch, in the hope that it would transcend to me being a top footballer, and therefore being able to have a relationship with the girl that I had a massive attraction towards.'

'Over time, it became a huge drive for me. More than anything else I've ever had in football. It led to me training harder that anybody I knew. At school, before school, after school, it really didn't matter. I was dedicated to finding ways in which I could be inventive and improve my footballing abilities. During this time, I'd absolutely be in the flow. It's almost meditative, to an extent, because you're just playing for hours and hours without realising how much you're learning, all driven by the desire to please and achieve my 'why' at that moment in time'.

And that, for Rich, is everything that the sacrifice and challenge comes down to.

'It just comes back to understanding what you're playing football for. Why are you putting yourself on that pitch, week after week, with all the potential pitfalls of embarrassment, injury, relegation and dejection that might come with it? Why are you putting yourself through one of the most performance-driven and merciless careers that there is? You'll only go above and beyond to produce and deliver the best possible standards in yourself if you've got the 'why' from within to motivate and inspire you.'

ACTION PLAN

There are a number of tools that we can use to try and understand this balance a little better, and we recommend keeping a daily reflective journal or performance handbook to keep track of how your life is going. You could ask yourself some questions along these lines:

How did you feel today when training?

Why did you feel this way?

Are you achieving enough rest and recovery from your football?

What is preventing your rest and recovery time being even better?

Are you looking forward to football sessions?

Why?

How physically and mentally tired do you feel?

What factors could have contributed towards this?

Do you need to adjust my balance at all to remain motivated for the game?

SECTION #4
PLAYER PROFILES

BEN FOSTER
Premier League goalkeeper and England international

CLARKE CARLISLE
Former professional footballer and PFA chairman

AIDY MARIAPPA
Premier League defender for Watford

BEN FOSTER
WBA GOALKEEPER

Your journey into football was slightly unorthodox… How did you get into the professional game?

Like many youngsters, Ben left school at the age of 16 and went straight out into the world of work, without any great idea about where his path may take him. 'Even at the age of 16 and 17, I wasn't taking football particularly seriously. I played for my local U18 team, who were the feeder club for a semi-professional side as well, and everything was just pretty relaxed at this point.' Even by his own admission, Ben was no great goalkeeper in his early years, and so that makes his late surge into the game even more remarkable.

During his time with the U18s, however, opportunities started to emerge and, one way or another, Ben was starting to build a little bit of a name for himself within the game. 'I managed to work my way onto the bench for the reserve senior side, which came as a bit of a shock, but soon I found myself as their first-choice: the previous number one was too old and had hung up his gloves!'

'About halfway through that season, having played quite well with the reserves, a combination of injuries went my way and I had an opportunity to play for the first-team proper. The rest of that season went incredibly well, despite there only being 15 or so games remaining, and I ended up with a number of scouts from all sorts of different clubs watching from the sidelines. A number of rumours went through the club that a couple of teams were going to put in a bid for me, and eventually I ended up signing for Stoke City for around £5,000 plus add-ons.'

We've spoken a lot in the book about pressure as a young footballer… Coming from a slightly different background, how did you find yourself dealing with the emotions of playing at the highest level?

'A lot of kids these days spend their lives dedicated towards being a professional footballer', says Ben, which actually may prove to be more harm than good for this aspect of their game. 'Many of them have been in academies since they were five, six or seven years old, with the dream always being to have made it as a professional. This can have an adverse impact on things because it ramps up the amount of pressure on them to succeed when they do finally get their chance.'

And Ben has certainly found his own way to deal with that pressure, or maybe he never had it in the first place… 'I'm 34 now, and even in the last couple of years I'm not really thinking about the game at all. Even as it's kicking off, there's no resemblance of fear or nerves in me, it just doesn't bother me.'

It's interesting to hear him speak so casually about the game, and this certainly supports some of Rich's stories from earlier in the book. There were still occasions, though, where the fear couldn't be shaken. 'That isn't to say that I've never had nerves: they've been quite prominent during big games or when we were in a relegation battle, but I can't say that they've been a part of my game that has held me back, and I also can't put my finger on why that is.'

In fact, Ben sees his nerves as more of an annoyer than anything else. To finish on a quote from the interview that sums up his approach to pressure perfectly: 'It [pressure] just did my head in, really. It wasn't something that was going to help me on the pitch so I was a bit annoyed to be laboured by it in my mind before the big games.'

You've had a couple of serious injuries in your career… How did you deal with these and bounce back stronger?

In this, and many other senses, Ben and Rich are of a very similar mindset. They are both driven towards making the most of the opportunities that come their way, even if they do not seem positive at first. 'I've always been the sort of person who's tried to go away when I'm injured and ensure that I come back even stronger, even bigger and even better.'

'When you're playing every week, it can be quite hard, actually, to keep improving yourself technically and physically: you can't go smashing those leg days to move things forward. Having an extended period of time (like eight or nine months for a cruciate ligament!!), you have a real opportunity to sit down, make a plan and put measures in place to make sure you maximise that time.'

As his career has moved forward, Ben also appreciates the systems in place to reduce chances of injury, and he works this topic into the interview, also. 'At the same point, as you progress through your career, you'll start to realise and appreciate what your body needs in a particular day. I know now that it's not good for me to be playing too much football. When I'm playing, I've got to really want to and enjoy playing, and it's great that I've got a club that looks after me, trusting me to know my own body and making sure that all the work we do will help me to maximise the quality of my minutes on the pitch.'

What qualities are required to become a professional footballer?

The million pound question: what traits do I need to be a professional footballer? There are clearly some massive strengths that Ben has to his game off the pitch as much as on it, and so we discuss these in some more detail. 'I think I'd definitely consider myself a positive player in terms of my self-talk and imagery pre-match. With every game that I play, I try and build a mindset of "I'm going to save the team today, regardless of what they might throw at us". It's that sort of attitude, that embraces the opportunity to succeed as opposed to hoping that a problem doesn't come my way, that I believe is really important to being the best player that you can be.'

'We see some of the young English goalkeepers coming through like Jordan Pickford and Jack Butland, and they look like they're on autopilot on the pitch, as if nothing could possibly harm them. There's no doubt that having that approach of "I'm going to kill it today, everyone will be talking about me after the game…" is the best way to go about it.'

In addition to this positivity and self-belief, there are other areas of the game that are just as important, believes Ben. 'Being a competitive person is a crucial part of making it as a footballer. You have to have a competitive nature, and always want to win, regardless of what it is you might be competing in. Like most other footballers, if I'm playing MarioKart with the lads, I want to win. And it's this same idea that has to transfer to all the different areas of the game if you really want to make it as a professional player.'

And it's not just winning in the moment, but also that constant search for development to improve and put himself in a better position next time. 'It does my head in if I don't win, and I'll end up having to go away and find a technique or method to improve and develop at whatever it might be so that I can win next time around.'

CLARKE CARLISLE
FORMER-PFA CHAIRMAN

What's the day-to-day life like as a professional footballer?

The question that every young footballer wants answers to, and one where Clarke's perspective gives a slightly different spin on the trials and tribulations of the game.

'I think that it's very hard within football. It's so performance-based that the wins and the losses come and are seen as by far the most important area. It's a part of the game that can be very hard to articulate to someone who hasn't been inside that environment.'

I ask Clarke if he can expand on any of these moments where he found the pressures difficult to deal with. 'There are little things, like playing small-sided games. You'll draw significance from who's team you are on, and this will contribute to your thinking of whether you're playing on a Saturday or not. It's one of the first wins and losses of a footballer's career.'

Beyond the match on a Saturday, Clarke knows that the chances are actually pretty thin, even for those within the game. 'There are in excess of 40 players in some squads these days, and you've got to make sure that you're one of the 11 that starts. If there are eight centre-backs, you have to be one of the two that is selected for the match. 'I think that it stretches further than that as well. To keep a balance between your own progress, commitment, and dedication to the sport, every single week, is a massive task, especially when you're then being fed with the rejection of not being selected because the manager has his favourite 11.'

'It's really hard to keep that in perspective, and not start to lose motivation. Given the amount that people give to get into professional football, not being picked on a Saturday seems like a judgement on your ability, and your identity itself.'

How did you deal with this within your game?

'I would say that I didn't deal with it very well at all', says Clarke, who has maybe picked up more press than most for the challenges he's faced off and on the pitch. 'It took many years for me to be able to distinguish that selection for my professional attributes from my value of a human being as feeling wanted.'

'I was validated by football: when I wasn't selected, it really hurt. I certainly took it home. It really made me question my worth in all areas of life, not just football. If I wasn't on the team sheet on a Saturday, then in all other avenues of my life (studying, working with other companies or just as a family member) my self-belief was absolutely struck to pieces and my behaviour reflected that. I'd stop contributing to conversations and just wouldn't want to engage with people in the streets because I didn't feel as though I was worthy of it.' An interesting, even if extreme, insight into the difficulties with self-esteem that some footballers can face. Always looking to move forward, though, it's what players can do to ensure that this doesn't happen that's most important.

Knowing what you know now, what would you do differently?

'In the context of football', Clarke asks 'why are manager simulation games so successful? Why are there 1.5 million players of The Sun Fantasy Football? It's because football is subjective.'

Clarke's thinking in this respect is certainly valid, as the sport revolves around the massively differing opinions that people may hold. 'One person picks Ronaldo, one picks Messi. It doesn't mean that the other one is worthless and shouldn't be on a football pitch.'

'That's what we have to remember in the team selection environment as well: it's just the manager's opinion on what best combination of 11 players will win the next football match. It's not even the manager's opinion on your abilities, or potential, in any sort of entirety. Being able to draw the distinction between who the manager picks on a Saturday and your own abilities and potential is vital. There are only a handful of players across generations who play any game, and your lack of selection might not have anything to do with your level of actual ability.'

How do you keep the motivation and inspiration when you are dropped to continue developing?

The final question that I put to Clarke considers how you can overcome, as opposed to prevent, the darker days in the game. His answer is learned and appreciative of the all-round nature of a footballer in the modern day. 'You have to understand and appreciate your whole self, in the context of life and outside of football. I've played over 500 games of professional football, but not one of those games made me a better father, son or brother. They merely showed my attributes in one section of my life.'

'You should be able to have the worst day at training ever, but know that when you come back tomorrow, you will still have the opportunity to apply yourself and try to improve once more. In the meantime, though, when you go home, you should be able to detach yourself and just enjoy your other human functions where you are valued, such as being a dad or chilling out watching TV.'

Still, though, there are a great deal of positives that can be built from playing football. 'It might give you some satisfaction, confidence or ego', adds Clarke, 'but it doesn't contribute to your overall being and existence in life. You have to understand that being a human being is not just being a footballer. It's about being a friend, a listener, a father, mother or whatever else it might be on top of that. You should be able to draw that distinction between work and life.'

AIDY MARIAPPA
WATFORD CENTRE-BACK

You had a bit of a rollercoaster journey in terms of how you came into the game... Tell us a little more about that.

Aidy's career as a youngster was one that ebbed and flowed at a great tempo. From being down in the dumps and out of the game, to playing in higher age groups when it wasn't so commonplace, his journey is a great starting point for understanding his advice a little better. 'At U15s, I was absolutely flying in my career. I was making appearances for the U17 and a lot of people around the game were talking about me. By the next year, though, everything tapered off and it all went to pot. There was a new academy director and he wasn't a fan of me, and the end result was that I didn't receive a scholarship.'

'The day I was told was horrible', remembers Aidy. 'I was in tears, really struggling to cope, and just sat in my room for hours on end, crying and wondering what to do next. We had a game with the U16s the next day, and I'm not sure I've ever felt the same burning desire to prove someone wrong as I felt that day. I was absolutely adamant that I was going to show my worth.'

When probed on why Aidy didn't manage to achieve the scholarship he'd worked for, the answer was probably resembling of a number of issues in talent development from years gone by. 'They told me in that meeting that I'd lost my pace and coordination, but I was going through a period of growth and maturation, so of course I was going to have lost some physical attributes, and this was very likely to impact on my technical ability as well'.

Moving forwards, Aidy got Man of the Match on his first game back with the U16s, and managed to keep drilling and work his way back into the U17 side, where he continued to pick up Man of the Match a number of times before the end of the season.

'I remember that they had a day when all the lads who were being kept on for the next year were called in, with their parents, and they did a bit of a lecture on what the plan was for the coming year and how the players could prepare for it. I was on a part-time scholarship at this point (the same as Ashley Young had had), but one of the senior coaches pulled my dad and I aside and said that they wanted to try and get me a full scholarship. I was ecstatic at this point, and massively hopeful that all of the work in trying to prove some of the individuals at the club wrong had paid off.'

The efforts were successful, and things started to pick up again when Aidy returned to the new season. 'As I came into the next year, with my full scholarship, I wasn't even involved with the U17s. Almost all the work I did was with the U19s during the week, and there was a massive focus and desire to every training session that I was a part of.'

'Many of the lads seemed to just come in to training to have a laugh and a joke, but that wasn't my scene at all. I was there to make improvements and be the best footballer that I could be. I already knew how it felt to feel like I'd lost everything, and I certainly didn't want to go back there again. Looking back, I probably could have lightened up a little bit, but that's the way it goes in football…'

What advice would you have for a young footballer?

A question that we've posed to all of our case studies, and Aidy focusses on some of the more difficult times in the game and how they gave him the burning desire to succeed long-term. 'For me, it took the depression of not getting a scholarship, a real low point, in order for me to bounce back and have that bit of hunger to show what I was capable of. That's all well and good, but ideally you don't want to let it spiral out of control to that level in the first place. What I always told my own kids is that you have to approach every day with the mentality of "what can I do to improve my levels of performance today?". If there's something you've got to work on, which there will be, go and do it.'

The passion, and raw tone, of Aidy is amplified at this point. 'Don't stop until you've made tangible improvements with it. As a scholar at the club, I took an awful lot of guidance and implicit feedback from guys like Rich and Ashley Young; I saw the hours that they put in and wanted to emulate that. Youngy would be outside practicing his free-kicks most days, whilst Rich would almost always be in the gym or out on the grass loading with plyometrics or something similar!'

Sometimes young players can get caught up in what exactly they can be doing to pick up these hours, and Aidy had some innovative approaches to improving his game. 'I would spend my whole summer in an athletics club, because I was so driven to get better. One of the real challenges for children in the modern day is that it can seem a lot more glamorous than it is, especially with the advent of social media. You need to understand that you have to stay head tough when times get difficult, and have the self-confidence to not accept criticism that's going to hold you back and not move you forward.'

CONCLUSION

ADAM WOODAGE AND RICHARD LEE

We started this book with the question, 'So, you want to become a professional footballer?'. At first, it maybe seemed just that: either you are a pro, or you're not. Without any real sense of differentiation between those who've made the grade and those who didn't. Over the past 120 pages, however, we've looked at a range of things that you might need to do in order to give yourself the best chance of making it to that top level. It's fair to say that the journey is based just as much on the mindset and attitude of a player as it is technical competence, especially in the sense of how they direct themselves towards continuous improvement, and hopefully this is a key message that you've taken from the stories and strategies that we have discussed.

Another idea that we have touched quite heavily on has been the importance of building blocks. It's a well known saying that Rome wasn't built overnight, and that's equally applicable to the world of football. Whilst there's certainly no harm in pushing yourself to those levels of physical and psychological capacity, you simply can't do it expecting to see results next week. Everyone develops at different rates, and will find different points at which they flourish and grow most noticeably. It's not to say that the player that develops earlier is in any way better than the one that takes another six months of graft and determination before they make their mark; the longevity and sustainability of their careers, instead, is what we seek to grade success by. So, even if things seem to not be going your way at first, it's vital that you trust in the process, build those strong foundations and keep working and working: you never know how close you might be on the day that you give up.

In the spirit of building blocks, and giving you one final piece of framework from which you can then go away and start to design your lifestyle, programme and plan to reaching your goals, turn the page to find Rich's list of concrete pillars to creating an athlete with the best possible chances of achieving success.

Set goals
Use process- and outcome-based goals to measure and motivate every step of your journey.

Find a powerful reason 'why'
Frame all of your motivations around this and use it to inspire.

Control the controllable
This is all you can do; trying to control beyond this will lead to frustration.

Reframe quickly and positively
Have that objectivity to understand a situation, and quickly adjust to improve.

Choose empowering beliefs
Beliefs aren't facts, so choose those beliefs that will help you move forward and generate positivity.

Appreciate the 'bigger picture'
Other people will have perspectives - try to understand and appreciate these to build your depth of knowledge and empathy.

Have flexibility in approach
Understand that everything you do, from goal setting to performance, must be ready to be adjusted should it not be working in a given context.

Improve communications
Stay positive both with yourself and those around you - it's another choice that you can influence.

Live in the present
Focus on maximising every moment of your present and future, because the past will take care of itself.

Eradicate excuses
Take responsibility, because excuses won't improve us - give yourself steps to improve next time.

Isolate thoughts
A thought shouldn't be held as fact; sometimes you might have to dismiss that which others choose to think of you for the long-term success.

Undertake continual improvement
Commit yourself to never ending improvement, because the benefits are invaluable.

Alter internal pressure
No one can put you under pressure, so use your awareness to reframe and choose a state the suits you better.

Twelve areas. An infinite number of possibilities for what they might mean for you. Keep pushing and moving forward with everything that you do, and we're sure that the results will reveal themselves, even if they're in a form far removed from that which you ever imagined. Remember, also, that if you have any questions on your road to success, any grey areas that you need guidance with or just a thought that you'd like some clarity on, we're only an email away and more than happy to support you and your goals.

Yours in football, success and the joy that football brings to so many across the world,

Adam and Rich.